A Hack in the Borders

Molly and Kate

A Hack in the Borders

Along the Offa's Dyke path

Dylan Winter

BBC BOOKS

Published by BBC Books,
a division of BBC Enterprises Limited,
Woodlands, 80 Wood Lane, London W12 0TT
First published 1991

ISBN 0 563 36288 X

Map by Eugene Fleurry
Photographs © Dylan Winter 1991

Set in Goudy Old Style by Ace Filmsetting Ltd, Frome
Printed and bound in Great Britain by Clays Ltd, St Ives Plc
Jacket printed by Belmont Press Ltd, Northampton

Contents

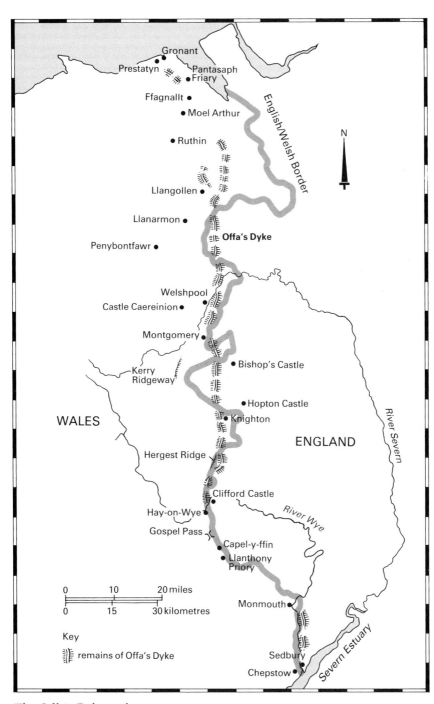

The Offa's Dyke path.

Chapter One

Waddling rucksacks, Civil War at Pontin's and a cow called Babe

An enormous rucksack, big enough to make a Sherpa wince, waddled purposefully across the wet sand of Prestatyn beach. On reaching the water's edge, its spindly white feet paddled a short way out into the greasy waves before turning around to face the sea wall where I was standing with Kate and Molly. The rucksack turned out to belong to a small lady who looked old enough to claim her bus pass. She was wearing the standard walker's uniform of bobble hat and anorak, her walking boots strung around her neck to keep them dry. Even though she was a good hundred yards away from me, I could see she was smiling. Not a 'Good afternoon, Vicar' sort of smile, but a full-blown, self-satisfied beam of deep inner contentment, of personal triumph. She stood there for a moment, waggled her feet around, then started to walk back across the sand towards the sea wall.

She was an unusual sight, but not really that unusual for this particular part of the beach at the eastern end of Prestatyn. This is where the 177-mile-long Offa's Dyke footpath finally meets the coast after snaking its way through the border region between England and Wales.

I almost envied that lady. She had finished what I was about to start, and she had done it the conventional way – on foot, and starting at the southern end near Sedbury Cliffs close to the Severn Bridge. I intended to start here at Prestatyn and get to the Severn Bridge on horseback.

To anyone with an ounce of romance running in their veins the appeal of such a journey is obvious: the simple life of the open road, the byway, the quiet countryside. And the beauty of it was that the horse would be doing all the work: I would enjoy the slow pace, the peace, the tranquillity of walking, without suffering the blisters and the aches. I would not even have to carry any gear because I had two horses, one to carry me and one to carry the little luxuries of life. As well as a tent and sleeping bag there was room for some good food, a half-bottle of Scotch, some books, my mouth organ. I would be able to enjoy all the advantages of walking, but none of the snags. Or so I thought as I found myself on a cool, wet day in mid-May on the beach at Prestatyn.

I felt rather alone, even though I had my two travelling companions with me – Kate and Molly, a couple of strong, healthy horses of moderate size and extremely mixed parentage. They were the sort of mounts no self-respecting Home Counties equestrian would be seen dead on, but hopefully they would be suitable for the job in hand. The younger of the two, Kate, was a big, almost black mare who was sold as just coming into her fifth year – quite young for a trip like this. Kate had a lot of carthorse in her: hairy legs and feet as big as a double-size deep-pan pizza. Sadly, a brain scan would be likely to reveal that there was no one at home. The only thing that could raise the faintest spark of grey-matter activity was the smell, sight or sound of food. She was what they call in the horse-dealing world a 'good doer', that is to say, she could survive and thrive on the sort of food that many horses would rather die than eat. Kate was willing to put her teeth around almost anything.

Molly, the other horse, was a very different animal but still rather too chunky for the Buckinghamshire hunting set. She was nine years old and should have been settling down to a calm middle age. I had bought her at an auction, which is generally considered to be a pretty risky thing to do. The sale particulars mentioned that she had been used as a hack, or riding horse, by an elderly gentleman who was now too old to ride her. This is the equestrian version of a second-hand

The start: Kate (left), Dylan and Molly on a wet day on the promenade at Prestatyn.

car being described as having been owned by an old lady who only used it to go to church on Sundays. When I bought her, Molly was as green as green could be. In her nine years she seemed to have done nothing and seen nothing. Anything and everything was a source of surprise to her. She looked upon the most innocuous items with suspicion – birds, cars, large bushes, felled trees, dead rats and sheep all had to be carefully scrutinised. But it was gates that were her particular fear. The odd thing was that if she approached a gate head-on she was fine, but whenever she passed a gate alongside the road or path she would start crabbing sideways away from it. I can only assume that at some stage in her life something nasty had come out from a gateway and given her a fright. Horses have long memories for things that have scared them. They can make elephants seem absent-minded.

I decided early on that because of her general skittishness I would have to use her as my saddle horse. That way, if she took a violent dislike to something and decided to take off down the road then there was a good chance that I would be going with her. She was just too unreliable to trust with the pack saddle loaded with valuable gear. Her saving grace was that she had a great curiosity about the world.

11

Kate would meekly follow the leading rein to wherever it took her – over a cliff or under a lorry, it was all the same to her. But Molly was always keen to find out what was around the corner. She was a natural traveller who really seemed to enjoy a journey.

Molly was also an indefatigable flirt. She loved other horses, especially male ones. A gelding would do, but if she caught a sniff of a stallion her tail would rise up to one side to expose her back end in a most undignified way. It was so embarrassing to be riding a mare which was constantly broadcasting come-on signals to other horses. Over the coming weeks I would be passing through some of the wilder parts of Britain, where stallions are allowed to roam free. This flirtatiousness was an aspect of her character in which I had a more than academic interest. I had been told that riding a mare when a rampant stallion is trying to do the same thing is most unpleasant.

Physically, Molly is a far finer-looking beast than Kate. She does not have that half-witted shire-horse look about her. She has a fine head and big, powerful body, just perfect for a large saddle horse any country gent would be proud to ride. The trouble is that she has stubby little legs. She is a good five inches lower at the shoulder than she should be to have really classic proportions. For me that made her just perfect. She has all the strength needed to carry my twelve stones – okay, thirteen – and is short enough to be easy to get on and off for the hundreds of gates I was expecting to deal with – assuming that I could get her close enough to them.

The start of a journey can be a bit of an anticlimax. The thing has been constantly in your mind and taking up much of your waking hours for weeks beforehand. It becomes built up to be something it can never be. Actually, it was a double anticlimax for me because I was not really starting until the next day. I had arrived in Prestatyn the night before, and planned to give the horses a day's break to recover from the five-hour drive from home. Today's three-mile round trip to the beach was to give the horses just a little bit of exercise, and to ensure that we had actually travelled the whole length of the Offa's Dyke path.

I had also agreed to meet Allan, a very nice man from Radio Wales who was going to interview me about my trip, at the symbolic start of the journey. While I waited for him to arrive I watched the old lady with the rucksack walk back across the sand. She sat on the bottom of the sea wall to re-lace her boots, stood up and walked past us. I looked in vain for any sign of surprise or curiosity in her expression at the sight of a rider with a packhorse waiting enigmatically on the beach at Prestatyn. She did smile in our direction, but then she was smiling in every direction – perhaps she had seen hundreds of horse-men with packhorses in tow on her trip up from the Severn Bridge. The smile on her face came from what was going on in her head, not from anything to do with the outside world. Perhaps it stemmed from a successful completion of the 177-mile journey from the Severn. Or perhaps she had had a few side-bets on with her fellow Tuesday morning whist-drivers and was heading off to collect her winnings.

It's funny how your mind wanders.

I decided to take the horses down onto the beach while I was wait-ing for Allan to arrive, in order to fulfil a long-held ambition of mine. Come to think of it, 'fulfil' is not quite the right word. My ambition had actually been to gallop a fleet-footed horse across a tropical beach and into an azure blue sea. Molly, Kate and the beach at Prestatyn fell some way short of that ideal.

The two horses behaved entirely to form. Molly was extremely reticent; she had never seen anything like a beach before, therefore it was to be feared. I urged her onwards, both verbally and with my heels. Eventually she did step off the concrete ramp onto the sand. Kate meekly followed in our wake.

Within two or three paces Kate put her head down and, after a perfunctory sniff at the sand, took a sizeable mouthful of it in the hope that it was edible. It failed even her sketchy gastronomic standards, and she spent the next few minutes going through an impressive repertoire of facial contortions in an attempt to get rid of the grit from between her teeth.

Kate, having decided to sample the sand on Prestatyn beach, found that it failed even her palatability test.

I urged Molly onwards and Kate dutifully followed, still making her bizarre facial expressions. Molly was even more suspicious of the sea and the waves than she had been of the sand. After a lot of urging, cursing and pounding of flanks I managed to get her within six feet of the lapping water, before she decided that enough was enough and that she would much rather be back on the safety of the promenade. I would not let her turn around so she did what she believed was the next best thing – she went into reverse. As we backed up the beach towards the sea wall some 150 yards behind us, Kate turned around and, still trying to get the sand out from between her teeth, followed. She, at least, was facing in the right direction. We eventually arrived back at the sea wall. Not for the first time, Molly had won and I had lost. I let her turn her head around to walk up the slope to the promenade. It was then that I noticed that the man from Radio Wales had arrived and had witnessed the whole ignominious retreat. I could hardly blame him for the opening question of the interview which was: 'Do you know what you are doing with these horses, Dylan?'

I mustered as much confidence as I could under the circumstances, and asserted that I did indeed know what I was doing and that I intended to take them down to the Severn Bridge, some 200 miles from where we were standing. Then came a much harder question. 'Why?'

My reasons were manifold. I wanted to make some programmes about the relationship between the English and the Welsh as it has developed over 2000 years of cross-border feuding, I wanted to do a long-distance horse ride, and I wanted a break from getting up at 4.30 in the morning to present *Farming Today*.

Allan turned out to be both a professional and a perfectionist. My first attempt at the interview was not to his liking, and he wanted to run it again. So we did. The horses started to get a little restless – Kate had nothing to eat and Molly was getting bored. Allan assured me that the second attempt was much better. Now, he asked me to get back up on Molly and ride noisily away. Getting up and getting going is always an exciting affair. Molly is one of those horses who refuses to stand still while you are climbing aboard. This is fine for Western films in which the long, lean hero casually throws himself into the saddle before riding off in a cloud of dust. However, I was wearing two pullovers and a coat, I had saddlebags to swing my leg over and I also had Kate's leading rein in one hand. As usual, Kate was ready to be off in a direction which might promise food, while Molly was simply ready to be off in *any* direction. There *have* been occasions when the two directions are one and the same, but this was not one of them. There was a brief period of disarray. After a suitable amount of shouting and cursing, I eventually got the three of us facing the same way and we clattered off down the promenade.

Allan seemed quite pleased with what he grandly called the 'sound picture' – but could I do it again and try to remember to say goodbye this time? So I turned the horses back. He wanted the sound of me actually mounting up so I had to get off. I got on again, said goodbye and rode away. He called me back saying that a passing JCB had ruined it. Could I do it again? And again? And just once more please.

Now horses are pretty stupid creatures, but they do know when they are being messed around. My departures became progressively noisier and fussier, with ever more clopping and shouting of 'Steady,

Molly' and 'Come on, Kate'. Allan seemed happier with each success-
ive re-enactment. I think he believed that if I did just a few more re-
run departures he might get something really exciting on tape. I was
beginning to believe he was right.

We said our real goodbyes and Allan drove away in his Ford
Escort. The speed, reliability, warmth and dryness of the car seemed
terribly attractive. An image of him sitting by his own hearth watching his own telly before going to sleep in his own bed with his own
wife snoring quietly at his side flashed briefly through my mind.
(Sorry, Mrs Allan.)

I headed off away from the beach along the road back towards
town. On one side is some rough salt-marsh pasture with a few sheep
and cattle grazing behind the barbed wire fence. On the other side is a
much higher, more formidable fence which marks the perimeter of
Pontin's Holiday Centre. It is not a thing of beauty – the fence, that is.
The holiday camp itself, with its military-barrack-style chalets and
aircraft-hangar main buildings, is no Taj Mahal either. The curious
thing about the fence is that the curved bit on the top faces inwards
rather than outwards. It is actually much easier to climb into the
camps than out of them.

To my untrained eye, the Pontin's Holiday Centre at Prestatyn did
look remarkably similar to the holiday camps of my youth. I was just
retreating into a reverie of memories when I heard a very un-holiday-
camp noise coming from inside the perimeter fence. It was the sound
of shouted orders and marching men. I watched with incredulity as a
group of soldiers emerged from between the chalet blocks and
marched around the perimeter road towards the main buildings.
They were wearing American Civil War uniforms. I stopped the
horses and Kate immediately put her head down into the sparse
verge as Molly and I took in the scene. The small band of forty men
were divided into two squads, one wearing the grey of Confederate
soldiers and the other dressed in Union blue. Following up the rear
was an orange Austin Allegro estate car, the driver of which was
wearing a fine Confederate uniform complete with a bright red

plume in his hat. It clashed violently with the colour of the car.

There was not much of an audience for the flag-raising ceremony. Apart from Molly and me there was just one man with a video camera which he was panning madly up and down the ranks. Watching his efforts on a TV screen would be a stomach-churning experience. There was one other potential witness – a bread delivery van driver. For some reason he was more interested in delivering his red plastic crates of plastic-wrapped, plastic white sliced bread.

Amid much poorly executed drilling and bugle-playing, two flags were raised – one Confederate, one Union. The shouting was generally of the highest quality, although the Allegro-driving Confederate officer did forget his lines at one stage and had to be prompted by one of the ranks.

Once the flags were raised, the colour parties fell in and the Confederate officer got back into his car. The strange procession marched slowly and noisily off. Molly and I stayed riveted to the spot as the group disappeared between the chalets. Eventually all we could hear was the sound of the two drummers trying to keep rhythm with each other. We listened on until the drums were quieter than the sound of Kate tearing at the grass. I felt sorry for the grass. To have struggled so hard to survive among the discarded Coke cans and sweet wrappers only to be cruelly uprooted, thoughtlessly masticated and then become part of the anonymous goo inside Kate's stomach was a sad way to end an existence.

The man on the main gate was a New Zealander. He did not seem at all surprised about being grilled by a man with a packhorse. He told me that it was the annual Pontin's Country-and-Western Festival and that everyone was dressed up as cowboys or Civil War soldiers. This coming Thursday they were going to re-enact the battle of Shiloh. I suggested that re-enacting the battle of Shiloh was an odd thing for a group of Brits to be doing. He shrugged his shoulders and said that he had been over here for two years now and nothing surprised him any more.

I took the horses back to the field above the town where I had left the tent and turned them loose to graze. As I walked over to the cattle trough to collect water to make myself a cup of tea, I noticed a fenced-off section of field and a smaller marker stone. It looked like a grave, but it seemed too large to be that of a human or a dog.

Later in the day, as I passed the farm on my way back to the field, after doing some last-minute shopping, I heard the thrumming sound of the vacuum pump coming from the milking parlour. I put my plastic bags of provisions down by the parlour door and called in to say good afternoon to my host. The farmer and his wife were just finishing off milking the last of their 100 dairy cows. I had spent half an hour talking to William earlier in the day. He projects the image of a typical hard-nosed farming businessman. He uses the natural assets of his farm to the full and is stoical about the various problems which afflict farmers in the 1990s.

I asked him about the grave in the field. He blushed through his weather-burnt face – and his wife Anne chuckled quietly to herself. He did not really want to tell me more, but I rudely persevered. As William stood there in the milking parlour between the bony backsides of his cattle, with the click-clack and sucking noises of the machinery going on in the background, the story unfolded and I came to see him in an entirely different light. The grave was that of a cow called Babe. William had bought her in the same year that he had got married to Anne. For some reason he liked the look of this particular young heifer as she was walked around the auction ring. He paid a terrifically high price for her – although it does not seem all that much now, some twenty-five years later. Babe had been on the farm ever since. Twenty-three years producing good yields of milk, always behaving well in the parlour and, possibly most endearing of all to a hard-pressed dairy farmer, never once needing the attention of the vet. William told me that she was remarkably affectionate. Most cows are pretty uninterested in the comings and goings of their human guardians, but Babe had an almost unnatural curiosity about people.

Dairy cows lead a pretty hard life. Pound for pound of body

weight, a milking cow is working as hard as a pre-war miner – the sort of man who spent his shift attacking the face with a pick and then shovelling the coal up into wagons. However, the miner only worked one eight-hour shift per day. The lactating dairy cow is doing this level of work twenty-four hours a day. She may look as though she is relaxing as she sits there chewing her cud, but her body is working like there's no tomorrow. When Babe got very old, into her twenties, William decided that she could no longer compete with the rest of the dairy herd, so he used her to suckle the offspring of the other dairy cows. Eventually he had to admit she was not only coming to the end of her useful life but that her quality of life was declining fast. It would be best for her to be put down. Cull cows are usually sent to the abattoir once they have run out of steam and, even at her venerable age, Babe's carcass could have been ground up into hamburgers and stock cubes and would be worth between £400 and £500.

'But I couldn't bear the thought of it,' William said. 'It's not the idea of people eating her – just what she might have had to go through before finally being slaughtered,' he added, before I got the mistaken impression that he was squeamish about eating meat. 'She might leave here on the Monday to go through a market on the Tuesday. It could then be Thursday before she got to the slaughterhouse, she might spend another day in lairage there. It would be Friday before I could guarantee that she had finally been dispatched. So I called in the vet and got him to do the job here. The vet's bill was another £25.'

After she had been put down, William and his son loaded her onto a trailer and took her down to the field where they had dug the huge grave with the JCB.

'Still, I expect you've got quite a few of her daughters in the herd now,' I said.

Suddenly the hard-nosed farmer returned. 'You know, that bloody cow gave me twenty calves and only three of them were females.'

To a dairy farmer who only wants female offspring from his best cows, that is probably the saddest part of the whole story.

I spent the evening reading in the tent, lighting one of the Long-Life Survival Candles I had bought specially for the trip when it got dark. I had found them in a specialist camping shop which was full of earnest men waving small weighing scales around and measuring every item they could get their hands on. The name of the game was to keep their luggage as light as possible but be ready to deal with any emergency. A rack of multi-function belt buckles was getting the young men very excited. The buckles doubled up as knives, can-openers, saws, two-inch rulers, screwdrivers and compasses. I imagined a keen backpacker having to hold up his trousers by hand, while the belt buckle did service cutting tinned sausages into precisely measured two-inch pieces before he cooked them over a fire which had been built south-south-east of his tent.

But it was the Long-Life Survival Candles that caught my eye. They came in a pack with a special camouflage design on the top, and I knew that I had to possess them as soon as I read the blurb on the back. 'Burns brightly for approximately 10 hours,' it said. 'Useful for light or to help start a fire. Can be used in any emergency for cooking or heating food and in its raw state can be of food value.' You would be ready to face almost any emergency with a couple of these in your pocket. I did try nibbling one, and I can report that it tasted rather 'waxy'.

By the light of the candle I surveyed the tiny space which was going to be my home for the next six weeks. It was supposed to be a three-man tent. All I can say is, they'd have to be very small and extraordinarily good friends. The obsession with multi-function belt buckles and edible candles became almost understandable. I was sharing the tent with a mountain of gear. For starters, there were the two saddles: one large military officer's saddle for me and another lightweight, but still bulky, pack saddle. Then there were six saddlebags, two large and four small. There was also a bag of horse feed and the tape-recording gear. Once all this lot was in the tent there was not much space left for me. It was like one of those children's puzzles made of a flat plastic frame with eight interlocking squares and a space for one more. In order to get one square to the right position, you have to go through a complicated procedure involving moving all of the remaining seven – some of them many times. Life in my tent was like that – except that I was the piece that had to fit into the last remaining square. It is just possible to play the game so long as you keep everything scrupulously well-ordered. If you unpack one item too many, chaos ensues.

I was tired but I did not sleep very well. I had made a couple of elementary mistakes when it came to pitching the tent. The keen backpackers in the camping shop would have been most amused: it turned out that I had pitched the tent where there had once been a building. Bits of rubble lurked malevolently just a few inches beneath the surface. Not everywhere, you understand, just where the tent pegs wanted to go. Some pegs were in the right place, but not in deep enough. Others were in deep enough but not quite in the right place. The tent did not have the crisp military appearance of the one on the illustration on the label. It was like the difference between the way mail-order clothes look on the model in the catalogue and the way they look on a real human being. By the light of my Long-Life Survival Candle, the walls billowed and crackled like the sails in a Hornblower novel.

I lay there remembering some of the many reasons why I prefer to avoid camping holidays.

A seasoned camper would have checked for the presence of builders' rubble before pitching his tent.

Chapter Two

Bathsheba's sinuses, Muscovy ducks and the disappearing river

Dawn came very late that first morning – about a year and a half late. As soon as I was up and dressed I gave the horses their morning feed and went over to collect some water from the cattle trough for the first of many cold-water shaves and washes. It was not an experience to be relished and one I would never learn to enjoy. It took me a good hour and a half to pack away all the gear, groom the horses and then load them up. Most of my impedimenta were stuffed into a pair of large leather pack-saddle bags. They are about the size of two medium-sized suitcases linked together with a wide leather band. I also had two pairs of conventional saddlebags designed to hang behind the saddle – the sort of thing you see John Wayne carrying from the livery stable to the hotel slung casually over his shoulder. John Wayne must be an absolute whizz at packing. It's amazing how much gear he can fit in: enough food for him and his horse for several weeks in the wilderness, a coffee pot, frying pan, two tin mugs, the shaving mirror to hang on the tree, a shaving mug, a razor and sharpening strap, a waterproof coat for the statutory downpour, a shovel with which to bury his best pardner and several enemies, a change of clothes for tea with the school marm and enough ammunition for prolonged shoot-outs with the Clinton Brothers, the Wild Bunch and three-quarters of the Cherokee nation.

During my practice trips around the block at home, we had looked a rather neat, well-organised little group – not exactly matching luggage, but not bad. Unfortunately I had not allowed for the spare tape recorder the BBC insisted that I took, and the eight battery packs, and the giant microphone designed to keep out the wind noise. All this extra gear had arrived on the day before my departure from home and it had to be safely stowed away. As a result, such minor items of comfort as the tent and sleeping bag had to be carried on top of the pack. They were stuffed into big yellow sacks with the legend 'Buckingham Builders Merchants' on the side, converting my oh-so-neatly arranged packhorse into a sort of four-legged bag lady with bundles of crackling plastic.

I was halfway through wrestling with the gear when Anne and William turned up to see me off. It was the first time that they had seen the horses. They liked them and said a few complimentary things about both of them – particularly Molly. Then they took a look at Kate. They both went rather quiet, and after a bit of whispering William asked me when the foal was due.

William was not the first person to suggest that Kate was in foal. When I had bought her back at the end of March, she had a fairly large udder on her and was slightly pot-bellied. I had asked the vet to check the horses over. He assured me that the horses were fine – a little overweight, but they would lose that once I started the trip. He suggested that Kate might well have had a foal the previous year, when she was still young, which would account for her udder and belly being rather stretched.

I explained this to William and Anne and they said that of course the vet must be right. Nevertheless. . .

Eventually I was ready and, after the usual disarray caused by the two horses setting off in different directions, I headed east out of Prestatyn, towards a village called Gronant. For the first time I felt that I was truly on my way. I actually knew where I was going to spend that first night. I had been up to Prestatyn by car the previous month just so that I could fix somewhere to stay for the first two nights.

The horses were fresh and stepping out nicely, and just for once they were walking at the same speed. Each horse has a 'natural' walking pace. For all her heavy, hairy feet Kate walks pretty fast. Molly, on the other hand, is a real tourist. She looks at things as she goes, slowing down to examine a sheep in the next field, or to eye suspiciously a tree stump. It can be extremely inconvenient to have a packhorse which keeps on overtaking the lead horse. But today Molly was keen to get on and Kate was following along, slightly behind and to one side.

The traffic on the road was light, and most people do actually slow down for horses – provided that they can see you. I am always at my most nervous just after having gone around a left-hand bend. Then any car coming up behind has very little time to see you. I knew that if any accident were to befall us, the most likely would be a car slamming into Molly's back end. Kate would probably be all right since she was always on the kerb side.

William had told me to take a road which ran up past the public house in Gronant. It was marked as being unsuitable for motor vehicles. Sure enough, as the road climbed up past the backs of the village gardens, the tarmac soon ran out. It gave way to a steep stony path

The way it should have been all the time – but wasn't.

snaking through the trees covering the hill up above the village. This was how I had imagined the journey would be – just me and the horses, their shoes clacking on the stony pathway.

It was a stiffish climb through about 600 feet over the two-mile length of the track. I took pity on Molly and got off to walk up. All three of us were hot and sticky by the time the path brought us out to a radio mast at the top of the hill overlooking Prestatyn and Colwyn Bay. I gave the horses a little rest while I took my last look at the sea. A lot would happen before I saw it again.

From here on, the track levelled out and eventually became a road, taking me through the first of what I came to think of as 'barking villages'. This one was called Gwaenysgor. As we entered its outskirts an invisible dog started barking madly at us. Then other disembodied barks from other houses and gardens joined in. A shock-wave of howls and dog barks spread out before us through the village. Many of the dogs could not have heard us at all, they were just joining in with their fellow members of the Gwaenysgor canine chorus. Although I heard scores of dogs I saw not one, and there were no human beings around either. I suppose that Gwaenysgor is a commuter village for people who work in Liverpool, Chester and Wrexham, which are now all within easy driving distance. To me it seemed a sad and desolate place. I am not sure the dogs liked it much either.

It had turned out to be a warm morning and the horses were getting hot. Around one o'clock I found a large field gateway and tied them up for a lunch break. I took off both the saddles to let the air get to their backs. The last thing I wanted was a saddle or girth sore to deal with. Before the trip I consulted a saddler from the Household Cavalry about the tack I should use. He told me that any saddle is a compromise between comfort for the horse and comfort for the rider. Most English saddles put the rider first and the horse second. The army, in his words, 'do not give a stuff about soldiers' arses, but we do care greatly for horses' backs.' He recommended that I buy a couple of second-hand army saddles, an officer's saddle for me because it is more comfortable, and a trooper's saddle to put on the packhorse because it is cheaper and lighter. His recommendation probably says more about the English class system than two or three issues of *New Society*.

The army uses heavy woollen blankets as a pad between the horse and the saddle; these are soon soaked in horse sweat which, if left to go stale, starts to smell horrible – essence of plimsoll and wet labrador. The cavalry troopers used to sleep under their horse blankets – they must have smelt dreadful. Every time I think of the love scenes in *Far From the Madding Crowd*, I think of Sergeant Troy and how bad he must have smelt. Perhaps Bathsheba had trouble with her sinuses.

After resting the horses for half an hour I loaded up and got under way again. Maps are not easy things to read when up on a horse and I did not consult it as often as I should. We took quite a few wrong turnings, but I had set an extremely modest target for that first day's ride, just ten or twelve miles. The farm I was heading for was a smallholding owned by a couple who had made enough money out of a transport business to buy some land and a modest house. They were farming in a small and uneconomic way, using the income from the lorry business to subsidise the farming.

There is a joke which celebrates the difference between farming and running any other type of business. I must have heard it told a hundred different ways at various harvest suppers. The story concerns a farmer who has won three-quarters of a million pounds on the football pools. He foolishly forgets to tick the box which asks for no publicity and finds himself on the local radio station. The inevitable question about what he intends to do with the money is duly asked. 'Just keep farming until it has all gone,' says the farmer.

On arriving at the yard I noticed at least half a dozen dogs, a huge number of chickens wandering around, a goat, any number of geese, turkeys, cats and, out in the pastures, lots of sheep. There were even a few white Indian ducks running around. These strange creatures are all legs and neck. They run around in groups or gangs in great excitement, like twittering, cackling, aristocratic schoolgirls with their heads held high and their elongated bodies tilted forwards.

There was also a group of three Muscovy ducks. These singularly ugly creatures have white bodies and red featherless heads – like web-footed vultures. They live off flies which live off dung, and catching flies requires lightning reflexes – from the neck up, anyway. From the neck down, these three were involved in some sort of prolonged slow-motion sex session – Muscovy ducks usually are. Don't know why, must be something in their breeding.

The mistress of this bizarre menagerie is called Marion. As she showed me the field for the horses, I remarked on the number of animals around the place. She said the sheep and the beef animals in the fattening shed were commercial activities, but the rest were just pets. It seemed to me that there were an awful lot of pets. I idly asked her how many. It was obviously a question she had never dared ask herself before. She stopped halfway to the gate, her eyes rolled upwards and she carried out a quick calculation: ducks (twenty-seven – soon to be a lot, lot more), dogs (six), peacocks (four), cats (used to be twenty-two but now down to a fairly stable eight following an extensive re-settlement campaign and bulk neutering session down at the

A rare shot of a Muscovy duck not engaged in some form of sexual activity.

vet's). And then there were the rabbits, turkeys and guinea pigs.

'About 150.'

I remembered William, my previous host. Despite his sentimentality over his favourite cow, Babe, he would not have approved of an agricultural holding with 150 redundant mouths to feed.

'Don't you eat the geese or turkeys at Christmas time?' I asked.

'Oh, they've all got names, I could never eat anything with a name,' she replied.

To people who have only seen turkeys plump, pink and plucked in a supermarket chill cabinet this is unbelievable. But looking at Marion's proud stag turkey and his little harem of females it was easy to see why he might stick in one's throat. Live turkeys have a rather endearing habit of joining in conversations – especially if someone laughs. A good human cackle may sound rather like a turkey gobble. If Marion or I laughed, a little wave of vocal appreciation would spread through the turkeys picking at the ground around us.

As I unloaded the horses Marion told me that she had an arrangement with her neighbour. The lamb in Marion's deep-freeze had come from her neighbour's farm and vice versa. When they have dinner together, the meat comes from Tesco's.

She eyed the horses appreciatively and mumbled something about how nice it would be to have a few of those around. I asked her if she would like to have a ride on one of them.

'Oh no, I wouldn't like to ride a horse, just look at it, just know that it was around the place.'

I told her a bit about the horses, and about William suggesting that Kate was in foal. Marion said that she had a neighbour, a man called Hughie Lewis who had worked his farm with horses until the advent of tractors. He was sure to be able to tell. She disappeared indoors to ring him up.

I had just got my gear unpacked and the tent up when the dogs and the geese put up a row in the yard. Hughie Lewis had arrived in his old Datsun pick-up. As he got out he growled at the dogs in a language they would understand. He hobbled across the yard – a scraggy rake of a man, several years past retirement age but with the look of someone who took little stock of the passage of time. He had a strange way of walking, like a badly manipulated string puppet, as though his legs were slightly loose in their sockets. The strange gait was accentuated by the way his feet rattled around in his oversize black Wellington boots. They had probably been bought too large to allow for several pairs of socks to be worn during the winter. Wet summer days are always a problem for country people.

Hughie was wearing a torn, terribly tattered sports jacket and a smile he must have borrowed from a much larger person. Despite the authentic-sounding low-pitched growl with which he had addressed the dogs, he turned out to have a high piping voice – but one which would occasionally plummet, completely out of control, down through an octave or two. I took to him immediately.

'Where are these horses, then?' he demanded. Marion and I conducted Hughie to the field where the horses grazed with the geese, the sheep and the goat. I called the horses over.

Hughie liked them a lot. 'Bloody good strong beasts,' was what he actually said. He ran his hands over both of them, feeling for faults in their legs, and found none. He lifted up Molly's feet and peered inside her shoe. 'Uh huh,' he said. The 'Uh' came out high and the 'huh' came out low.

He looked Kate over, walked around her, felt her udder and her teats, shoved his fist into her side, just behind the ribcage, and declared himself baffled. She was showing some signs of pregnancy but not enough of them. After a few more randomly pitched exclamations and mumbles, he said that she probably was not in foal, but even if she was she must be several months away from having it.

He told me about an infallible test I could use. The idea is to keep the mare in overnight and not give her any water. Then in the morning offer her the coldest bucket of water you can find. While she is drinking, hold your hand against her flank up under her ribcage. He said that the sudden cold water would make the foal shiver and you would feel it move inside the mare.

I was worried about working her if she was in foal but Hughie had no doubts at all. It used to be the custom to work a pregnant mare right up until the very last day and only then turn her out. Once she had dropped the foal she would be back in work within two days and the foal would be allowed to walk along beside its mother. I was a bit concerned how I would know when birth was imminent. Hughie had another infallible test. 'A mare will always wax up twenty-four hours before she foals,' he said. 'As soon as you detect a waxy deposit on her teats then you know that she is going to have it.'

I was hugely reassured on several counts: she was probably not in foal, if she was in foal she was several months away, even if she was I could keep working her right up until the last day, and finally her teats would tell me before she was ready to have it. It is marvellous how much these country people know. You can learn a lot from folklore. Bit of a shame that Hughie turned out to be wrong on nearly all counts.

We sat on a wall watching the animals. In front of us, the sheep, the cattle, the geese, the goats and now my horses were all contentedly grazing in their own way. It was a calming sight – like a tank of goldfish, only much, much better. I began to understand why Marion liked having her menagerie around the place.

The conversation between the three of us, three different generations, three different backgrounds, ebbed and flowed quite naturally. The noise from the animals died away as the sun disappeared. The talk turned to the ground and the way that it moved, tipping over dry stone walls for no good reason and bending what were once perfectly straight fence lines. Marion said that when she first moved to this house it had been possible to see every inch of it from the kitchen window. But over the past couple of years the dips and undulations had deepened and widened. There were now quite a few spots in the field where sheep could drop completely out of sight behind one of the ridges.

Hughie mentioned his badger field, which once had a river running through it. One day he came to check the cattle and found that the ground had opened up and the river had disappeared beneath the surface – swallowed whole. Bit of a shock when it happens in a field you have known all your working life. I mentioned that I would like to see that.

'Come at dusk and we might see a few badgers as well,' said Hughie. He threw the last bit of tea from his cup onto the ground in front of us, with a practised swirling flick which ensured that any tea leaves would depart with the dregs. But this is the age of the tea bag and such gestures are as redundant as the skills of the horse ploughman.

Later on that evening, as it was getting dark, I walked the mile or so towards Hughie's farm. My approach was heralded by the inevitably barking sheepdog, which was chained and snarling in the corner of the yard. A much kinder-looking bitch came timidly towards me, her tail wagging uncertainly between her legs. Hughie emerged from a shed in the yard saying that he was just doing a 'spot of tidying'. I could see inside the shed behind him and there was a fair amount of tidying to be done. Junk was everywhere. There had once been work benches along three walls, but these were now piled with rubbish. In one corner there were literally hundreds of glass bottles – mostly lemonade and sheep drench rather than alcohol. They were stacked so high some had fallen off and smashed on the floor. Hanging from a rafter were a few sheepskins, *sans* heads but with hooves still attached. There were lumps of metal everywhere, some recognisable as tools, hammers and crowbars, others more difficult to identify. The whole lot was covered with a layer of dust which rounded off the edges of everything and brought a satisfying harmony of shape and colour. Somehow Hughie had been doing his 'spot of tidying' without disturbing the dust.

All Hughie's junk had a purpose or at least a meaning, he said. Some of the bottles contained useful things (one had petrol in it, but he seemed unsure which). The sheepskins were useful for keeping sick animals warm. They had, he claimed, saved many a heifer from dying after a difficult birth and saved the cost of a vet's bill. The pram which was hung in the rafters was the same one his mother had wheeled Hughie in some seventy years before.

After the tour of the shed and its treasures, Hughie declared it time to go to the badger sett and we walked down the darkening lane to the field beside the house.

We went through a typical, badly-hung gate which needed lifting to swing it open. I mentioned that you do not come across many well-hung gates in Wales.

'Better not to,' said Hughie. 'People will only swing on them. Better to have the bottoms firmly on the ground to make people climb over them.'

On the way across the field Hughie showed me the river. It was eerie to see it in full flow and then suddenly disappear into a hole in the earth like bath water down the plughole. Hughie pointed his torch down where the water was disappearing. You could not see the bottom. He had lost an animal or two down there before deciding to leave the field to the badgers.

Hughie and I sat and talked quietly as the last of the light faded away. Actually, it was more a case of Hughie talking while I listened. He told me about his farming career, about how agriculture had gone wrong with too much nitrate, too many medicines and too few people.

When I suggested that he was just against progress he denied it. He had bought a Ford tractor in 1938 and got rid of all the horses just as soon as he could. 'Spent too many hours walking the fields staring up a horse's arse,' he said.

Hughie had no children and was obviously worried about what the future held for him. I suggested that he had not prepared very well for his old age. He seemed slightly offended and told me that his whole breeding policy over the last fifteen years had been tailored for his retirement. He had been producing a flock of easy-lambing ewes which would not need much in the way of looking after. They could look after themselves and be perfectly happy outside all through the year. Hughie had been having trouble with lambing recently. He had

suffered a spate of lambs presenting with one leg tucked back underneath themselves in the womb, which meant that he had to be there
to assist at lambing. He could not work out why this should be happening, until he began to notice one of his tups and the way it had a
habit of lying down in the field with one leg tucked under it in an
awkward way.

'Took it straight down the market the next week – never had any
lambing problems since.'

Hughie talked and I listened until well after midnight. I never saw
a badger but I did learn a lot: about overcrowded cities and the way
that society was breaking down in them 'just the way it does in an
overcrowded rat burrow'; about mad cow disease and the way that
man has 'buried nature, we've buried nature, that's what'; how the
companies that produced the pill caused the AIDS outbreak and
have now gone on to make more money out of selling condoms in
different flavours ('what does someone want with a condom fla-
voured with pina colada?'); about worming dogs by letting them eat
rabbit skins and worming sheep by undersowing a new crop of grass
with mustard seed. A picture began to emerge of a man whom life
had not treated particularly well but who was still optimistic about
the future. A man who had always hoped for the best from people
and was willing to give them the chance to prove themselves but then
was not too disappointed when they turned out to be less than
perfect.

I also learnt of Hughie's plastic hips and the way that one night he
woke up with a terrific cramp in his legs only to find that one of them
was bent back underneath him. Somehow in the night it had come
out of its socket. He had thrown back the quilt ('continental quilt,
mind you') and dragged himself across the bed. His plan was to put
his foot against the bed head and somehow push the plastic ball back
into its steel socket.

'There was a terrific crack, like the sound of a gun, and it went back
into place. Lucky, wasn't I? Wasn't I lucky?'

Chapter Three

A rich blend of muck, stifle slip and monks in Ford Escorts

Kate is always easy to catch, even in Marion's field with all the distractions provided by the sheep, goats, geese and turkeys. Just a rattle of a food bowl brought her barrelling over as though she had not had a scrap to eat for a week. Molly was a bit harder. She always submits eventually, although in the early days of our relationship she was a real pain. She had a habit of staying just out of range and would even circle some ten or twelve feet away refusing to be cornered. The skill and length of the performance was always greatest when there was an audience. I noticed that Marion was watching from the kitchen and Molly had decided that today she would practise her whole balletic repertoire. It was a full five minutes before I managed to corner her by the water trough.

I tied the horses up to the fence to eat their breakfast while I went back to the tent to have mine. Camping breakfasts are miserable affairs – no toast, no cereal, no fresh milk, no fresh juice. It was down to the cheese, dried fruit and water biscuits.

After this unsatisfactory meal I packed the paraphernalia away in the saddlebags and went out to see to the second part of the horses' morning routine – a thorough brushing. Real horse people consider a good grooming to be a 'thoroughly good thing'. Not to do it would be to break all the conventions.

I think that horses enjoy the sensation of grooming, and it makes me feel as though I am doing something for them in return for all the work they put in on my behalf. One thing that all this grooming has done for me is to make me happier about horsehair sofas. I never understood where the Victorians got enough horsehair to stuff all those sofas, let alone all the other items of furniture it was used for – chairs, railway seats and so on. But seeing the huge quantities of hair that Kate and Molly produce during the course of an average grooming session, I no longer worry. At her peak in the spring, I was harvesting at least a bucketful of horsehair every morning from Kate alone. I am sure that she would produce enough for a chaise longue in a year.

The grooming does force you to inspect the whole of the horse from head right down to hind feet. You can spot any cuts or grazes before they cause problems. And horses are host to the most horrendous range of diseases and disorders. I was foolish enough to read an equine veterinary book before leaving on the trip. The names of some of the afflictions have the ring of an ancient curse, and I scared myself silly by reading about the likes of dropped elbow, laminitis, navicular disease, pedal ostitis, ringbone, sandcrack, seedy-toe, semoiditis, stifle slip, stringhalt, thrush and dishing. And that was just the chapter on feet and legs.

Once the horses had been groomed, I turned my attention to their feet. The vet had told me that if any problems were going to arise on this trip, it would be foot problems. Horses' feet are hard around the edge but soft in the middle, and little stones, flints or slivers of wood can make their way up into a foot and make the poor animal lame for weeks. The vet suggested that I check their feet at least three times a day. But first you have to clean them out. Now many people believe that a hoof pick is used for removing stones from horses' hooves. In fact, ninety-nine times out of a hundred, what you are scraping out of a hoof is a highly compacted version of what drops out of a horse's bottom. This is not surprising, as the horse leaves little cairns of the stuff all over the field. On this particular morning Marion's mixed grazing policy had given me an interesting blend of half a dozen different types of animal excrement to scrape out. This is one good reason for having breakfast *before* you groom.

Every morning, the horses' hooves yielded a rich blend of several different brands of . . . Definitely not a job to be done before breakfast.

Then it was time to load up. It was to be a fairly short trip to my next overnight stop. I was to head for a place called Ffagnallt, which is marginally more difficult to pronounce than it is to spell. Other Welsh linguistic challenges in the area included Rhes-y-cae, Lixwm and Mwccwd. The sun was shining and it threatened to be a warm day. Marion had suggested that I should stop off at the Franciscan friary at Pantasaph where I should arrive about midday. She told me that it would be a nice place to rest the horses and I might even get a cup of tea from the Brothers.

Kate's girth seemed a little tighter than usual, but I was sure it was my imagination playing tricks following the previous night's talk with Hughie Lewis. The horses and I left at about ten in the morning, just as the day was starting to warm up. I could not see any way of getting to Pantasaph Friary using bridleways, and I was still a little nervous about how the horses would react to heavy traffic, so I took a large detour around a short section of main road.

The minor roads in Wales are no great trauma to travel on. An hour or more can pass without meeting a car and the landscape is quiet, green and undulating – good fertile land which was well worth fighting over, as the English and the Welsh had done for hundreds of generations. It was a hot day and the horses and I were glad of the shade provided by the mature trees along the verges. The route took me along the side of a terribly ordinary-looking ditch which was clearly marked on the map as being part of Offa's Dyke. Many archaeologists would contest whether or not Offa's earthworks ever got this far north. My route took me through Pant y Wacco and Gorsedd and into Pantasaph, where the map showed the presence of both a Franciscan friary and a convent – although I am sure that everything was completely above board.

The friary church was built of light grey stone and looked like any other Victorian House of God, except that it was too large for a village, too small for a town. The buildings were extensive and all built in the same style as the church with tall windows and steeply pitched roofs. It was surrounded by the same strong trees that had lined my route. There was a huge car park with its own one-way system and a visitors' centre at the front. I almost did not go in, but it was a hot day, the horses needed a rest and I do like looking around churches. They are cool and quiet and invested with people's hopes and sadnesses.

I found two trees which provided suitable shade, nourishment and a secure anchor point for the horses, and I removed their saddles. Then I went and sat on one of the many benches around the place just to watch them for a few minutes to make sure that they had settled down. It was very quiet except for the sound of the birds chirping somewhere in the branches above my head. The heat was shimmering on the tarmac of the car park, but it was lovely and cool under the trees.

Kate made a start on the grass around the base of the tree. Molly stood and looked around for a bit before starting to rub her head on the trunk of her tree. She had her bridle on and was damaging the leather so I went over and put her head collar on instead. Travelling with horses is not the relaxing experience it is cracked up to be.

The peaceful air of Pantasaph eventually soaked through to the horses' brains and Kate gave up on the grass and the succulent spring leaves on the lower branches of the tree and fell asleep. Even Molly started to get drowsy. The place had that soporific, southern Mediterranean siesta-time feel. Within minutes, both horses had settled down with no sign of movement from either of them save the occasional laconic flick of a tail.

I walked over to the main entrance of the friary and hauled on a lever to the right of the door. A bell sounded deep in the building. Footsteps came padding quietly towards the door and a heavy key was turned in the lock. I prepared to tell my story to the hooded and bearded figure which I confidently expected to see. Instead I found myself burbling incoherently at a young woman dressed not in a habit, but in pastel shades of blue, and wearing white sandals. She listened without surprise to my brief explanation of my trip and then calmly informed me that the Brothers were down at the cash-and-carry.

I told her that I had expected to be greeted by a man. She laughed and told me that her name was Celia and that she was one of a pair of identical twins who worked at the friary running the office for the retreat centre. She told me that the Brothers would be back soon and that I could wait for them if I wished. I should keep my eyes open for a red Ford Escort. I picked up a couple of booklets from a side table and went out to sit on my bench again. They were hardly the religious tracts I had expected. One had the look of a time-share brochure, heavy on pictures, thin on words. The glossy illustrations showed lots of ordinary-looking men doing ordinary things such as drinking tea, repairing Land Rovers, rotovating vegetable patches and singing a lot. The ordinary-looking men were wearing brown habits with long pointed hoods hanging down the back and white cords around the waist. Poking out around the necklines were rather bright un-monkly-looking shirts with overlong shirt collars. Some of the little tableaux had a rather posed, slightly uncomfortable feel to them, as though someone had arranged the Brothers in attractive little groups carefully balanced to show a generous age range and skin colour. In one picture a Brother was wearing an incongruously chunky diver's watch while he looked on lovingly as a colleague played a guitar. Throughout the brochure the words 'Accept the Challenge – Dare to Dream' were printed in large letters on every page.

The friary had caused quite a stir and not a little bad feeling when it was established in the 1850s. The local landowner, Lord Denbigh, decided to have a big Anglican church built at Pantasaph to celebrate his recent marriage. Building churches is a slow business so Denbigh and his wife went off on their world tour while waiting for it to be completed. Unfortunately the Denbighs, who had left Britain as staunch Anglicans, came back as devout Catholics. While they were away they had decided to give their new church to the Franciscan friars.

The local Anglicans, who were rather looking forward to taking over their nice new church, were not a little upset at this change of heart. In fact, they took it all rather badly. A civilised air-clearing chat around a table proved to be impossible so everyone involved retreated behind legal barricades and started lobbing lawyers at each

The peace and quiet of Pantasaph Friary soaked through to the horses and they were soon dozing peacefully in the shade.

other. Christians are no better at peace-making than anyone else. Eventually the High Court in London decided that the Denbighs could jolly well do whatever they liked with their church, and in 1852 the first Capuchin friars arrived to a pretty cool reception from the locals.

The friary at Pantasaph was now being used as a religious retreat where thirty guests could be kept in comparative luxury with comfortable beds, continental duvets and *en suite* bathrooms. The rates appeared to be reasonable at a 'donation' of £17.50 full board. Should you wish to book in advance for the retreats, then a registration fee of £10 has to be paid. 'The deposit is non-returnable and is part of the total offering.' Delicately put, I thought.

After half an hour or so the promised Ford Escort arrived and two men started unloading food into the visitors' centre. One of them, a strong, clean-shaven, balding man, was wearing brown trousers and a brown pullover. The other, a much slighter individual in his late thirties with an over-carefully trimmed black beard, turned out to be Brother Stephen. He had a brightly checked shirt collar sticking up from the neck of his habit. I helped them unload the car and, as I did so, expressed my surprise at being met at the door by Celia. This prompted the first of many laughs from Brother Stephen, who evidently found the world a hugely entertaining place. I explained who I was and that I would like to talk to them about the friary and what it was for.

Brother Stephen said that he could certainly spare me the time and also offered me some tea while we talked. We decided to sit outside under the tree where I could keep an eye on the horses. Brother Stephen started telling me about St Francis – the man who started a religious dynasty which has lasted almost a thousand years. He called him Francis, in the way that you might talk of a friend who has just nipped off down to the shops. Brother Stephen painted a picture of a man with all the frailties and inconsistencies most of us recognise in ourselves.

Stephen said that St Francis was an impulsive sort of person. He

Brother Stephen, who claims to be pessimistic but is still full of hope.

was the son of a nouveau riche Assisi cloth merchant. He became a knight and was kept in Perugia as a prisoner of war for two years before being baled out by his father.

'One day, after his return home, Francis was praying in the local church – which was a pretty run-down sort of place. He heard God calling on him to rebuild the church. Francis took his father's best horse, loaded it up with his best cloth and sold the lot. Horse and all. He used the money to repair the church roof.

'Milk with your tea?' said Brother Stephen, almost as though it were an integral part of the story. For a second or two my brain struggled with trying to fit this curious comment into the narrative. All I could manage was a confused nod once I had remembered the tray of tea things in front of us. Brother Stephen gave one of his laughs, sharing and diffusing my embarrassment with it.

'As you can imagine, the father was not best pleased and he clapped Francis in irons for a while, but his mother let him out.

41

'The trouble is,' said Brother Stephen, pausing only to offer me the sugar for my tea, 'Francis could never get over the fact that God had become man, and then could not get over the fact that he had been crucified, and then could not get over the fact that he came daily in the Eucharist at Mass. His whole life was spent trying to come to terms with the enormity of God's actions and what man had done and was doing in return.'

Stephen talked a lot about St Francis. Two particular incidents stuck in my mind. On one occasion Francis was travelling with a friend. The two of them had not eaten for days and were sitting on a rock feeling pretty glum about things. Suddenly Francis started praising the Lord. His companion asked him what on earth he had to be thankful for. Francis told him that he was thanking the Lord for the rock they were sitting on. Another time, much later, when Francis had established his first friary, one of his Brothers found some money and kept it. Francis decided to punish the Brother and told him to go and preach to the people wearing only his underpants. Later that day, Francis felt bad about what he had told the Brother to do, so *he* went off to preach wearing just his underpants, to punish himself for punishing his Brother.

I said that Francis sounded as though he were slightly deranged – possibly as a result of spending two years in chains. This comment elicited another long delicious laugh.

'Francis has a different sort of sanctity from the British version. People like Thomas More or John Fisher always have a very moderate, understated quality. But Francis was always one for the dramatic gesture.'

Then the subject of poverty came up.

'Francis was convinced that Christ was absolutely poor, possessing nothing, so he tried to follow Christ's way of life, and we are trying to follow his,' said the Brother, who was sitting in the delightful setting of a few million pounds' worth of real estate in one of the most beautiful parts of the British Isles. We were drinking tea provided by the Franciscans. If Brother Stephen really had been following the life of Francis or Jesus, I would have met him on the road and have been offering him my tea from the pack lying under the tree beside a dozing Kate.

This prompted the longest laugh of the day.

'The trouble is that we have this vow of poverty and rich people keep on giving us things, like this friary here at Pantasaph. Compared to some of the places they have in Italy this is a mere hovel.'

And then came that laugh again, this time with a hint, not much more than a hint, of self-mockery. I asked him about it. He seemed to find some rather sad things really quite funny. 'We have to laugh, life is not serious. The great mystics say that when they reach the heights of mystical union, whatever that means, at the centre of heaven there is laughter, which makes absolute sense. Well, it does to me, anyway,' he said.

Brother Stephen had been a Franciscan since 1981. He joined after abortive careers as a painter, a teacher, an archaeologist and a singer. He seemed slightly disillusioned in a way. He had joined the Franciscans presumably to get away from the complications of a property-owning life, and here he was running a large retreat, employing staff like the twin sisters, rushing off to the cash-and-carry, having building works done in the friary to provide the guests with central heating, continental duvets and hot and cold in every room. He added to the stress in his own life so that stressed people could come here to recharge their own batteries. When we went indoors to take the tea things back he offered to get me some more books to read. I could hear his sandal-flapping, key-jingling, rosary-jangling and door-slamming progress fading through the friary as he rushed to get the books. A second or two later I heard him making his equally noisy return. He did not conform to my preconceptions of what a holy person should be. He was running his life at double speed to allow others to slow down.

I asked Brother Stephen whether he was optimistic for the future. He did not answer me at once, perhaps because he was slightly out of breath, perhaps because he wanted to think.

'No, I am filled with hope,' he said, 'but I am not remotely optimistic. I think that it is all going to fall around our ears. We are going to witness the collapse of civilisation and a resurgence. It has got to collapse before it can get itself right. It appears we are on a downhill spiral, determined to destroy the planet, cutting down rainforests, and the way we treat animals is extraordinary. We are cruel to the environment, we are cruel to animals, we have abortion laws which are preventing people from being born and presumably we will soon have legalised euthanasia. Sometimes I think we are on the way to autogenocide.

'I think there will be some new leaders to show us the way, people like Mother Teresa. It could be the Pope, but the poor man gets a horrible knocking and he has the Vatican to deal with and all the horrible problems of its finances. I always think that if you got rid of all the Vatican art treasures you would destroy the Italian tourist industry.'

The mention of the tourist industry reminded me of Lourdes in France where so many sick and infirm go to be healed. It rather unsettles me to see so many people going to be cured and so few coming back any the better. Brother Stephen's answer made me feel better about the place.

'People are not cured; they are healed. I know that sounds as though we are having our cake and eating it, but you see miracles *do* happen. I have seen them, I have been involved. I would never say I healed anyone – God heals them – but I have done things and things have happened. I remember a fine friar, I wanted him to pray with me because I had a Hebrew exam the following day. My Hebrew was appalling, absolutely terrible. I did not have a hope of passing the exam. This Friar John was very charismatic, a fine man. We were going to pray about this exam and suddenly a very good friend of mine rang up and said, "My cousin's baby is dying of meningitis, there is something wrong with the brain, the heart has stopped." So I said we will go and pray about this. I went back to my room and John was sitting on the bed looking at a picture of Christ on the desk, and suddenly he said, "The Lord has given this child its life."

'So I went off and rang my friend back and said, "The Lord has given this child its life."

'I said it with more confidence than I actually felt and she said, "But is it going to be all right? The X-rays say there has been brain damage."

'I said, "Perfectly," and I thought, well I hope I am right.

'And I was, and I passed the Hebrew exam. I got a lot from God that night, didn't I?'

And I got a lot from Brother Stephen that day – much more than just a cup of tea.

Chapter Four

The Charge of the Light Brigade, fig rolls and badger baiters

After leaving Brother Stephen to his hectic life running his holy hotel, I returned to the horses. Molly was awake and watching but Kate was dozing and quietly snoring. Her lower lip had drooped right down, making her look even more vacuous and low-bred than usual. I re-saddled the horses and we walked off down the one-way system at Pantasaph Friary. The road to Brynford took us over a bridge across the main A55 trunk road. Molly did not like the sight, sound and smell of the lorries pounding underneath us but she seemed to be calmed by Kate's total lack of interest in them.

The horses were turning out to be better suited to the job than I had any right to expect. Neither of them was fussy about either food or water. They behaved themselves when tied up and, most important of all, they were both well up to the weight I needed them to carry. Kate was only carrying about 120 lb – a horse of her type could easily carry a rider twice that weight. But the inert mass of a pack is much worse than a rider who will balance and move with the horse. A pack tends to sway from side to side, which is much more tiring for the horse to carry and greatly increases the chance of saddle sores.

In carrying me and a couple of largish saddlebags, Molly was having to carry a lot more weight than Kate, although it was Kate, as packhorse, who got all the sympathy and sentimental 'aaahs' from people we met on the way. I am quite a big person, six foot tall and tubby enough to be reticent about removing my shirt in public. Add to my twelve and a half stone the weight of my clothes, the saddle and the two saddlebags and Molly was probably carrying close to 200 lb.

Unfortunately with horses their physical characteristics are only half the equation. What is going on between their ears is just as important. The trouble is that they are not really that clever. Dogs are much more intelligent when it comes to problem-solving or having a sense of fun. Dogs seem to be able to enjoy a joke with a human being. They know when you are playing a game with them and generally know when to stop. But then dogs have been domesticated for a long time – far longer than horses. Dogs also have a much better natural understanding of a co-operative venture. In the wild their survival depended on being able to work together and hunt as a pack. Understanding what is going on in another animal's brain is, and always has been, an essential survival tool for a dog.

Horses are of a different psychological make-up altogether. They seem to care little for people other than as a source of food or pain. They either can't tell, or don't seem to care, what sort of mood their human companion is in.

The thing to remember about a horse is that, given the slightest chance, it will always let you down. As soon as the wicket gets the slightest bit sticky, the first animal to be clearing out is the horse. The dog will stand by you, or at least cower behind your legs, thereby

The plastic bags started to proliferate and the horses' neat packs started to grow.

demonstrating some faith in your ability to resolve the problem. If you are lucky it may even stand beside you and get ready to fight on your behalf. The horse has no such faith in humankind. It will assess the situation as being entirely hopeless and hightail out of the area. A horse can see or imagine danger in places and objects which neither you nor a dog would ever notice. A dead cat at the side of the road or a nun with a pushchair would have a horse leaving the scene before you could say Roy Rogers. Horses are to the animal world what insurance actuaries are to humans.

Horses are extremely good at blind panic: their main survival tactic is to run very fast in the opposite direction to anything that might be a threat. They have developed two very effective rules for survival. Rule one is, 'If in doubt, run away.' Rule two is also fairly simple: 'If you see someone else running away, then jolly well join in and start running in the same direction, just in case they are right.' Some hopelessly idealistic people suggest that the way horses behave in battle gives the lie to this. How can such a timid beast bravely charge into enemy guns? Talk to any cavalry man, if you can find one still alive, and he will confirm that the hardest thing about a cavalry charge is stopping it from turning into an uncontrollable stampede. I am not sure that there was all that much equine bravery involved in the Charge of the Light Brigade. The horses were not running gallantly towards the enemy. Lodged firmly in 600 diminutive brains was the idea that 599 other horses could not be wrong and must surely be running away from something infinitely more frightening than these foreigners with cannons. Try making a one-horse cavalry charge and see how far that gets you. But for rule two writ large in all those primitive equine brains, English history would have been cheated of one of its most glorious cock-ups. The gallant 600 was, in all likelihood, 600 men pulling as hard as they could on 600 bits firmly clenched between 600 sets of teeth belonging to 600 terrified cavalry horses whose minds were focused on an imaginary danger behind them somewhere.

Unfortunately the modern world is full of things which look as if they might attack horses – JCB diggers, umbrellas and wind-blown Tesco carrier bags. Despite all its shortcomings, a horse is a delightful form of transport. The view from on top of a horse is brilliant. It is the double-decker bus of the countryside where everything looks somehow different, somehow better. You get an improved sense of perspective. Horse travel is also quiet, sedate and environmentally friendly. Rabbits, deer and birds all but ignore you. Foxes run away, though – bit of a shame that. But horses are designed for travelling in the countryside, not for dealing with main roads and juggernauts pounding under bridges.

After crossing the A55, with Molly's eyes carefully following every lorry passing under the bridge, the road took us out across one of the worst golf courses I have ever seen. There was a lot more rough than green, and what little green there was looked pretty scrubby. There were a few golfers playing a round or two but they must have been outnumbered forty to one by sheep.

The route then took me through by Bryn-Mawr and through the Halkyn Mountains. The topography makes no geological sense with gullies, mounds and ponds all over the place. The whole area is riddled with old mine-workings – an ideal location for a science fiction film. The locals have been using the old shafts to dump household rubbish. The council has now blocked off most of them, but the place is still littered with discarded sofas and mattresses.

A mile or two further on we passed a quarry where twentieth-century man is doing his bit to change the landscape. In the bottom of the quarry were half a dozen of the diggers loading rock into lorries for moving away. The yellow machines must have been lifting several tonnes of stone with each bucketload. Each of these digger drivers was moving several thousand tonnes of rock a day just by shuffling the little red, white and yellow-tipped levers in his air-conditioned cab while listening to the sound of Radio 1. Their predecessors, working a few miles and a couple of hundred years away, would not have been able to move as much material in a lifetime of sinew-straining work.

Eventually the bleak rocky terrain gave way to more fertile tree-covered scenery as we came down off the mountain and into the valley bottom. Ffagnallt Farm is owned by a brawny dairy farmer called Pete, who plays the part of the hard man but underneath is as gentle and protective of his family and friends as he is of his cows. The farmhouse has a legend, a ghost and a fragment of the skull of Dafydd, Prince of Wales, sitting on the mantelpiece above the fire in the front room. Actually it is only the skull which sits on the mantelpiece. No one has ever seen the ghost except for a mad maid who is the main character in the legend.

As soon as I had seen to the horses and pitched the tent, Pete and his wife Sue asked me in for tea. The kitchen is typical of many farms – part sitting room, part office, part canteen; the real hub of the working farm. In the hour I sat there with them, the phone rang half a dozen times on farm business, someone came over to borrow a tractor, a fertiliser rep called and the kids came back from school. In between this lot Sue told me about the house and the skull. She had known about it before Pete had even shown her the farm and had told him that she would only be prepared to live there if the atmosphere was right. In the ten years they have been at Ffagnallt she has felt nothing unpleasant at all. I am sure that she does not have time to notice creaks and groans in the night.

She took me through to the front room. There on the mantelpiece was a small glass-fronted box, eight inches square and three deep. Lying on a piece of 'Shades of Pastel' tissue paper was a fragment of skull, orange-brown in colour and slightly shiny. It could easily have been a piece of pottery save for the characteristic 'stitching' where two of the cranial plates had come together and the ridges over the eye sockets. It was small enough to rest comfortably and unimpressively in one hand.

The story has it that if the skull is removed from the room bad luck will befall the household. The legend says that, at some time in the past, a maid working at Ffagnallt fell out with her mistress. In a fit of pique, after the rest of the household had gone to bed, she grabbed

50

the skull off the mantelpiece and threw it into the pond beside the house. Later that night the family awoke to a terrible row. The maid was standing in the pond with the fragment of the skull in her hands. The family coaxed her back inside but she refused to let go of the skull. She was a gibbering wreck for two days before they got her to talk any sense. The maid said that she had heard screaming in the night and had been driven from the house by hands dripping in blood.

Quite how a lump of Prince Dafydd's skull finished up in the front room at Ffagnallt no one now knows, but Sue was taking no chances. When I tried to coax her outside the house to be photographed in front of the pond holding the skull, she refused point-blank and said she would try to prevent anyone else from taking away the skull – just in case.

The skull on the mantelpiece at Ffagnallt Farm was supposed to have been that of Dafydd, Prince of Wales.

The clear skies produced a very cold night and the deficiencies of my sleeping bag became all too apparent. I had been persuaded by the salesman in the camping shop to go for an extremely lightweight model. The label said that it was filled with duck down. The label is wrong. The sleeping bag was nowhere near filled; I doubt whether it was the full production from even one duck. It may have been very light and compact, but it was pretty useless. I finished the night wearing my socks, cords, tracksuit bottoms and a couple of sweatshirts; and I was still cold. I dropped off just in time to be woken by the dawn chorus at about 4.30.

The next day I left the horses at Ffagnallt and walked up to the hill fort at Moel Arthur. This is one of half a dozen major forts which are concentrated along a single eight-mile stretch of the Clwydian Hills.

I wanted to go on foot because that is the way that the locals would have travelled when fleeing from raiding parties. The first part of the walk was along narrow country roads with high grassy banks on both sides. The lanes would block with snow as soon as the first flakes drifted across the fields. The vertical verges were already well populated with spring flowers. Given a couple more weeks of this good weather they would be delightful. This was how roadsides used to look before the advent of the granular fertiliser spreaders which chuck pellets of nitrate into the field margins, making the soil too fertile for wild flowers to compete with the grasses and cow parsley.

I had been told to sneak in and have a look at what the locals called the 'secret garden'. It is just off the road through a gate and into a piece of woodland. It has been created by a couple who live in a block of flats in Liverpool. I did not really know what to expect – a patch of grass, a few vegetables perhaps. What I found took my breath away. It had once been a small quarry of some sort. A 150-foot-long curved rock face was covered in plants which tumbled down all over it. Formal flowerbeds had been made down at ground level. There were also a few flowering shrubs and a beautifully flat, well-manicured lawn. A lot of love had been poured into this garden. I would have liked to meet the people who made this little sanctuary.

This minor gardening diversion put a temporary halt to my attempts to think myself into the minds of the people who lived in this area 2000 years before as they ran, panic-stricken, towards the hills. The map showed a nice easy footpath going right up to Moel Arthur. It was presumably the same route which would have been used by both refugees and attackers. It went past the house which used to be owned by England football captain Kevin Keegan. Damn! Another distraction, and another reminder that this area is within easy commuting distance of Liverpool.

The map told me that the climb up to Moel Arthur was about 900 feet. My feet and my lungs told me that it was a good deal more than this. If I was fleeing from raiders, I would be prepared to carry only my most prized possessions.

As I continued on up the hill and the slope got steeper, I realised that a few of my most prized possessions might get jettisoned on the way. The plus side would be that any attacking army would also have been thoroughly exhausted by the time that they got to the top. I am not sure that I would be prepared to climb a hill like this and fight the defenders just to get my hands on their valuables. I would content myself with burning and pillaging the homesteads. It took me about two and a half hours to climb to the top of the hill. All the way up the skylarks were singing despite the strong wind. It seemed rather incongruous. Skylarks in my home county of Buckinghamshire save their singing for hot, windless days. Welsh ones cannot afford to be so choosy and obviously have to have a much more robust attitude to the weather.

I thought that Moel Arthur would also be worth all this climbing effort because it has more than its share of legends. First there is the grey lady who misdirects travellers. She is supposed to be Boadicea. Quite why an East Anglian queen should choose to spend her after-life hanging around a Welsh hill fort misdirecting travellers is a mystery. There is also some buried treasure and a few nonsense stories about King Arthur who was supposed to have had a palace up here. Arthur, if he ever existed, was supposed to have been active in about

AD 700 , some 500 years after the hill forts fell into disuse – but why let historical fact stand in the way of a good legend?

Once on top I found a few unimpressive ridges and banks surrounding the summit. I sat down to eat my lunch in the lee of one of the ridges, thinking that if this was the best preserved of the hill forts on the Clwydians then I was glad that I had chosen this one. I am sure that I would hardly have noticed the existence of the others. The view was great, but these anonymous lumps and bumps failed to produce any sense of history. I looked down the hill to the fertile land below and tried to imagine the Saxons or the Romans pillaging my home. I failed. My mind kept on wandering around thinking about Kevin Keegan's hairdresser, why blisters had suddenly appeared on my feet, and how they manage to dry fruit without it going mouldy and whether they bother keeping flies off it. I started looking for black specks on my dried apricots. I turned my attention to the rest of my lunch – cream crackers and fig rolls. Just a few more reminders of the pleasures of camping.

The combined effects of the sun, the sound of the skylarks and the previous night's sleep deprivation caused me to nod off. Something woke me up and, in that confused stage between sleep and wakefulness, I became aware that I was no longer alone. A short woman, dressed in a yellow anorak, was walking purposefully around the site. I could hardly ignore her as we were the only two people within five miles, so I said 'Hello' and offered her a fig roll. She turned out to be an archaeologist called Margaret Worthington from the University of Manchester Department of Extra-mural Studies. She was planning on bringing a group of her students up to Moel Arthur later in the summer and was making a quick advance recce of the site. I asked her to practise on me. Margaret managed to transform my impressions of the bleak lump of Moel Arthur. She walked me a few yards downhill from the crest and asked me to imagine the lumps twice as large as they are now, as they would have been before 2000 years of rain and wind and frost smoothed them off. Then to envisage a ten- or twelve-foot-high wooden palisade on top. Now imagine trying to attack by running uphill through a barrage of arrows and other missiles. She showed me where the gateway would have been; even now the ramparts at this point were a good twelve feet above our heads on either side, and in those days they would have been even higher. After the gateway the entrance curved in and around to form a narrow passage through which any attacker would have to pass. The defenders would be high above their heads on both sides. The presence of the wives and children in the compound behind would have lent ferocity to the defence. It was hardly surprising that the marauders went in for raiding rather than siege warfare.

Most of the time there would have been just a skeleton 'garrison' here. There is plenty of evidence of metalworking going on up on the hill forts. The men stationed there may have kept themselves busy with making swords or shields or bearings for cartwheels – in effect, a standing army of blacksmiths. The fires of their forges would have shone out at night as visible evidence to any would-be attacker that the fort was occupied by strong men.

In the space of twenty minutes, her enthusiasm and knowledge turned what had seemed no more than a grassy knoll into what it really was, a crucial part of the development of British civilisation. I hoped that her students would appreciate the lesson as much as I had.

On returning to Ffagnallt, I found there were several horses there, apart from mine. One of the horse owners, called Tim, turned out to be a member of the local badger group – a diverse band of people who have decided to do something positive about the problem of badger baiting rather than just sit tut-tutting over their Sunday newspapers. Twice a week, Tim and his wife Genette either ride or drive over to a nearby sett to make sure that it has not been disturbed by baiters. They were due to go over that evening and invited me along, so I saddled up Molly and joined them. It was a very pleasant ride along the lanes and bridle paths. It was nice to just ride and not worry about slipping packs or keeping on the right path.

After an hour's ride we arrived at the badger sett. We tied the

Badger-minder Tim, looking for spraints (little packages) left by his charges.

horses up by a farm road and Genette stayed to keep an eye on them while Tim and I went over to check the sett. He asked me to keep quiet and not to talk as he led me across to a small patch of woodland occupying a steep bank in the middle of some sloping pasture land. I assumed that he did not want to disturb the badgers, but in fact it was to avoid disturbing any baiters who might be there. Inside the wood the bluebells were in full flower, their pure translucent blue a stunning natural colour contrast to the bright green of the new leaves on the trees. Up high on one of the trees was a sign warning any potential baiters that the badger sett was checked at irregular intervals both day and night. Tim told me that badgers tend to stay in setts and seldom abandon them no matter how much they are disturbed. This one could well have had badgers in it when the Clwydian hill forts were still in use 2000 years before. There were plenty of setts with their wide curved entrances and areas of compacted earth in front. Tim showed me a couple of large depressions where the badger baiters had dug into the sett, and an even larger one which had been dug out to form an arena in which the badger would have been forced to fight the dogs. Badger baiting obviously required a lot of hard physical work by the people involved.

'Our aim is just to make sure that it is not worth their while taking the risk of coming to raid the setts,' said Tim. The previous Easter, he and Genette had caught some baiters actually at the sett. 'It was a very still day and we heard the sound of the shovels before we came anywhere near the sett. I checked to make sure that it really was baiters and sent Genette back to ring the police. I took a few photographs of the men and then went back to the road to wait for the police to come. I did not want to leave them digging; I wanted to protect the badgers, but I knew that it was more important to get a successful prosecution. I had to brief the police on the sort of evidence they would need to collect.

'The police arrived within four or five minutes of being phoned and I took them in from a different direction so that we could get as close as possible without being spotted.'

Tim pointed to a hedgerow about twenty feet above the sett. 'We stood there for a couple of minutes watching the bastards before they noticed us. It was great to catch them like that.'

The standard legal defence from the baiters is that they have been digging for foxes. They will sometimes bring a fox carcass with them as proof that it is a fox earth and not a badger sett. This lot had brought along a dead fox, but it was still frozen, having been brought out of the deep-freeze only that morning.

The men had to keep digging after the police had arrived because one of their dogs was still underground. They eventually recovered it – still attached to a badger. The dog was badly bitten around the face.

If the police had not arrived then one or more badgers would have died – either at the site or taken away in a sack where a much bigger audience would have been able to enjoy the sport of watching a badger being torn to bits by dogs.

Tim told me that in badger-baiting circles females, or sows, with young cubs are the most highly prized. Their willingness to fight the dogs in an attempt to protect their young makes much better 'sport'. The early spring is the peak period for baiting. If they find a sow with cubs then it is common practice to break her back legs with a blow from a shovel to give the dogs a better chance.

The group of baiters caught by Tim and Genette had come in from Blackburn – a good two hours away by car. They were successfully prosecuted for illegal digging and were given the maximum fine of £1000. Fining is the norm, although in 1990 one group of baiters was sent to prison. However, their offence was cruelty to dogs, not to badgers. Fines do not generally bother baiters as they are usually settled by their Terrier Clubs.

'How badger baiters can come to a place as beautiful as this, with the oak trees, the flowers, the birds singing, and only want to dig some poor little beast out of the ground is beyond me,' Tim said angrily. 'They're scum and if they come here they won't be safe. We'll be watching for them.'

Chapter Five

Infidelity with Gwillum, Isobel Barnett and a friar's death

Leaving Ffagnallt was a wrench; the people at the farm had been extremely kind and welcoming. For the first time I would be travelling without the security of a guaranteed place to stay. I had been on the road for several days but I had been hopping from refuge to refuge. This was really it.

The route took us along quiet leafy farm tracks where the trees made bright green translucent tunnels for us to pass through. Here was the sort of quiet not found in the Home Counties where you are never out of earshot of an engine of some type – be it a jet, a lawn mower or the distant buzz of a major road. Just the sound of the birds and the hooves of the horses as they thumped across the turf or clattered against the odd stone. Eventually this gave way to the growing sound of a clay-pigeon shoot. It was inevitable that the spell had to be broken in some way.

The tracks eventually took us out into a pass through the Clwydian Hills where the bulk of Moel Arthur loomed above us. The day before I had climbed up to it the back way. Viewed from below, the strategic importance of the hill fort was obvious. We made good progress during the first four hours and eventually came down off the bleak open scenery of the hills and into the lushness of the Vale of Clwyd where we stopped for lunch at the side of the track. I felt rather lonely as I reloaded the horses and made a start on the remaining four miles to Ruthin. My plan was to find somewhere to stay on the Llangollen side of the town so as to get a good start for the next day's journey. An hour later I was skirting Ruthin and starting to look seriously for a suitable field.

The next farm looked promising with a few paddocks around a small bungalow. There were two horses in one paddock and the others had plenty of grass. I tied Kate and Molly to the fence at the end of the drive and walked up towards the house. There was a large cement lorry parked in the drive near the house, and hanging on the garden gate was a sign saying 'Beware of the dog'.

I never know what such signs are supposed to be telling me. Am I being advised not to enter the garden at all, or only to do so with caution – perhaps having taken the care to arm myself with a big stick first? On this occasion there was no dog to be seen.

The kitchen window was open and I could hear a man and a woman engaged in animated conversation. At first I thought that it was one of those radio plays where two people stand beside a kitchen sink and argue with each other – usually in Northern Irish accents. These people had Welsh accents and at this stage it was still a long way short of an argument. It was just a couple of people scoring points off each other.

I tried an experimental 'Hello'. Then I hazarded a louder one. I rather hoped that the dog I had to beware of would hear me and alert the two people. No such luck. I tried a quick 'Yoo-hoo', which is just as stupid a noise as 'Coo-ee' but is somehow more masculine. Still no response. Nor any sign of the dog. The conversation in the kitchen took a turn for the worse and appeared to be centred around the absence of the man on the previous night. It made compulsive listening.

It emerged that the woman had not led an entirely blameless life in the past either. At one time she had enjoyed a brief dalliance with someone called Gwillum – her own brother-in-law, no less. Mentioning the name of Gwillum was not a good move. It further soured an already difficult relationship. I also learnt during the course of one exchange that the man should never have 'done what he done to

*The lanes were so quiet that lunch
stops could be taken anywhere.*

Gwillum'. Presumably this was some sort of revenge attack for what
she had done with Gwillum. I was fascinated and terribly embarrassed at the same time – and also slightly scared. Here I was, seventy-
five yards up a complete stranger's drive, listening at a kitchen
window to what was by now a no-holds-barred domestic row in
which all the juiciest and most sordid details were being brought to
the surface.

What should I do? Should I keep on trying to attract their attention? They would hardly be in the mood for welcoming a stranger
with two horses onto their property. I could retreat, but the drive was
in full view of the kitchen window. If I walked back down it there was
a good chance that one of them might spot me slinking away. The
Gwillum-basher might decide to come after me – and there might
still be an unpleasant dog around somewhere.

I decided that a discreet retreat might be worthwhile, so I turned
my back and walked down the drive, trying to inject a note of non-
chalance into my walk. Whenever I think about the way I walk, it all

goes wrong. It's like coming through customs. It is a mystery why I'm never stopped – I radiate guilt. I had an uncomfortable feeling in the small of my back, as though bracing myself for attack. It never came. I just remounted and rode away wondering what the people would make of the two piles of horse manure and the heavily grazed bit of hedge at the bottom of their drive.

A mile or so on along the road I came to a large field full of bulls of the most splendid variety of shape and colour. They ranged from the slightly bony black-and-white dairy sires to the golden-coated and massively muscled Continentals. There must have been 150 of the one-tonne monsters carefully spaced out across the fields.

The bulls were individually tethered to large steel contraptions designed to allow them to graze their own patch of grass without coming into contact, and therefore confrontation, with each other. They had rings through their noses and chains running up and around their horns, which had been cut off square and stuck out of the sides of their heads like second sets of ears. The tethering system meant that some parts of the field were grazed terribly short while others had not been touched at all that summer and were too long. The effect was to make the place look rather messy.

In the past, each of these animals might have been patriarch of a harem of thirty or forty cows – master of all the mistresses he surveyed and serviced. Now, thanks to the modern miracles of artificial insemination, each of these monsters could be the sexual partner of half a million cows. They could be the grandfather to millions. Yet every single one of them was a virgin, and had probably never been within sniffing distance of a cow since he was first taken away from his distraught mother at two days old to stand lowing and bawling disconsolately in a tiny calf pen with only a rubber teat for succour.

Now, in their maturity the bulls are 'milked' two or three times a week, and the valuable product of their loins carefully parcelled up into tiny five-millilitre portions and plunged into liquid nitrogen until needed. These bulls can go on siring offspring long after they themselves have declined into dog meat.

In the early days of artificial insemination it was common practice to use a 'teaser cow' which would be penned up in a special box. The bull would be taken to her and, as he jumped up on her back, a man would rush forward and divert the bull's penis into an artificial cow's vagina which had been thoughtfully filled with warm water so as to avoid putting the bull off his stroke. Bovine sexual intercourse is not a prolonged business and within seconds half a pint of semen would have been collected.

The experts eventually realised that it was not necessary even to use the teaser cow – a teaser steer, or castrated male, was employed instead. Now even he has gone and a cow-shaped trolley with a hide securely attached to it is used. A man holding an artificial vagina sits inside the artificial cow on one of those orange or grey plastic seats you find in schools or colleges. I suspect that his occupation would have brought a furrow or two to Isobel Barnett's brow on *What's my Line?* had he ever been invited onto the programme to mime his occupation. I decided that I would not even bother to stop and ask if I could stay the night. The Milk Marketing Board is a bureaucracy. Bureaucracies are seldom hospitable.

Eventually I came to a large house with a nice piece of parkland in front of it. The grass there was long and lush but the field was too uneven and had too many trees for it to have been shut up for hay. I rode the horses up the drive, tied them to a tractor harrow in the yard and asked if I could put up in the field for the night. The lady there said that I could but that the fences were not in a very good state and some were made of barbed wire. I assured her that my horses were well used to barbed wire and that there was so much grass there that it was inconceivable that they would make a bid for freedom. I offered to pay and this seemed to clinch the deal.

I unloaded the horses by the gateway, led them over to show them the water trough and then let them go. I then set about looking for a suitable spot to pitch the tent. I wanted the shelter of the trees but did not want roots to interfere with the tent pegs. The perfect spot was about seventy yards from where I had dumped the gear. Next time I would find the best place to pitch the tent *before* unloading the horses.

Within an hour I was lying on my bed watching the horses through the tent door. I decided to have curried noodles for supper and delved down into my plastic bag of food – only to find that it was sticky and slimy inside. I sniffed my fingers to try to identify the contaminant. Freshly-broken egg does not have much of a smell. The problem lay at the door of yet another useful little device I had bought at the camping shop. It was an impulse buy. They had them beside the till. Never buy anything which has been placed beside the till. It's bound to be overpriced or useless or both. This object was a dinky two-seater blue plastic 'crush-proof' egg box – only 99p. The idea of my two eggs safely cocooned in it, like twins in a womb, was most attractive. I remember hearing the man behind me in the queue sighing and tsk-tsking as I picked it up. At the time I wondered what he was so unhappy about. I now know that he was discreetly vocalising his disapproval at my naive amateurishness. Only an idiot would buy such a thing.

I emptied all the food out of its plastic bag and started trying to clean the egg off. It would have been quite easy with the help of lots of warm, soapy water, but the task was quite beyond the powers of my wet tissue. I feared that there was enough egg left to start smelling bad in the coming weeks.

The noodles looked very nice on the packet, with bits of carrot and green pepper mixed in. Once the water was boiling, I tore the top off the packet and poured the noodles out into the pan. They had suffered on the journey. What came out was a powder that would have done credit to a McDougalls flour-sifter. There were not even any bits of bright green pepper or orange carrot to spoil its uniform oatmeal-coloured perfection. The noodle flour was followed by a foil sachet which I delicately fished out of the boiling water, blowing on my fingers while I looked again at the picture on the packet. I ripped the top off the sachet and poured the contents into the fawn-coloured scum in the pan. Still no festive bits of red or green. In vain I tried to reconcile this mush with the picture on the packet.

The noodles tasted as bad as they looked, but I was prepared: I had brought some curry powder with me. A teaspoon of it put some zing into them. Actually a quarter of a teaspoon would have put in more than enough zing, but I was at the bottom of a very steep learning curve. I contemplated the culinary delights which awaited me over the coming month as I spooned the mulligatawny porridge into my mouth.

I fell asleep soon after supper but was woken again some time after midnight by an owl in the trees above the tent. I lay there for what seemed like hours listening to the quiet noises of the countryside – the horses grazing near the tent or the cattle in the field next door, the occasional bleat of a distant sheep. I was just dropping off again when I heard a dog barking in the distance. It was echoed by dogs on the neighbour's farm, then the dogs at this farm started up. It was not a frantic bark communicating fear or warning. It was carrying some other message as it rippled across the countryside. I wondered how far it had travelled, how far it would go. As it ebbed away to the south I turned on the radio for a bit of company, but there was only Cliff Richard.

The dawn chorus saw to it that I was awake well before the sun came up. I decided that a town breakfast was needed. It turned out to be a good mile into town from Cefn-coch, where I was staying. I passed a hotel on the way in. The kitchen window opened straight onto the pavement and the waft of cooked breakfast was like a wall across my path. I could taste the food. I walked on seeking more humble places to eat. I asked the first person I met whether there was a café open, but Ruthin could only offer a tea shop which did not open its doors until 10 a.m. I thought of filling myself up on Mars bars and Coke from a newsagent, but could not face it. So I walked back to the open window of the hotel kitchen, leaned in and asked the chef about breakfast. A few minutes later I was in the panelled dining room with a massive and hideously unhealthy breakfast on a plate in front of me. It felt odd sitting there with the sales reps and American tourists but the breakfast was worth every penny of the £3.50 it cost me. I felt so civilised sitting up at a table rather than crouching on the floor of the tent like an animal.

When I tried to pay, it turned out that the receptionist had nipped out for a few minutes. The chef suggested that I should drop by later in the day and pay – not the sort of trusting courtesy you could expect to receive in the cynical Southeast. Feeling pretty good about the world in general, and about my trip in particular, I walked up towards the centre of town. I began to understand why there were Americans in the hotel dining room. Eugene and Mira could photograph each other up against any of the half a dozen buildings which surround the town square. To the people of Minnesota every one of them exuded 'history'. These buildings were once important as the powerhouses of local government. Now they have been taken over by the banks and building societies. They still exert influence over the way we run our lives but their power comes from a source other than public consent.

It was another warm day. I really was enjoying more luck with the weather than I deserved on this trip. The sun was shafting in towards Barclays Bank which occupies an imposing building on the western side of the square. In front of the bank is a large boulder which stands about four feet high. On the other side of the square there was a bench with three men sitting on it. If people have time to sit on a bench they usually have time to talk, provided that you have a story or two to offer in return. We swopped a few. The rock turned out to be at the centre of a classic piece of Arthurian mythological rubbish. It seems that King Arthur had a friend called Huail. They were both in love with the same woman – not Guinevere, the old men assured me. Arthur and Huail fought long and hard over this woman. The fight ended inconclusively, save that Arthur had a badly gashed leg which caused him to walk with a slight limp for the rest of his life. In the afterglow of a good scrap, Arthur made Huail promise not to tell anyone else about what had happened and how he had acquired the limp.

Time moved on and one day Arthur was travelling through enemy territory here at Ruthin. He was supposed to be in disguise but Huail recognised the limp. The two of them decided that they had enjoyed the last fight so much that they should have another. This time Arthur won and beheaded his former friend on this very stone. Well, that is what the old men told me anyway. At times I feel almost sorry for Arthur, if he ever existed that is. His name seems to attract all sorts of idiotic stories.

As I was leaving the square I noticed a sign set high up on the wall of a building. I almost did not bother to read it. The notice said that the building used to be the courthouse. A portion of the town gibbet, last used in August 1679 when a Franciscan friar was hanged from it, can still be seen projecting from the wall. I stood there and stared. The image of Brother Stephen, his humanity, his generosity, his laugh, his singing voice, his love of God and people was still very much with me. I just could not envisage a society which could hang someone like that. I wanted to know more about the Franciscan friar who had died in the town square 300 years ago. Ten minutes spent in Ruthin town library revealed that he was a man called Father Meehan, an Irishman who had gone to Rome to be trained as a Franciscan. In the summer of 1678, a year before he was executed, he was on his way home to Ireland where he planned to spread the word of the Lord. His boat should have sailed straight from France to Ireland – both good safe Catholic countries. Unfortunately, he was shipwrecked off the Devon coast and decided to go overland to North Wales to make the short sea crossing home from there.

He had almost made it to the coast and safety when he was picked up in Denbigh – about ten miles north of Ruthin. He had dropped his bag in the street and some papers had fallen out. It was a bad time for a Catholic to be travelling through Britain. Titus Oates was stirring up anti-Catholic sentiment and accusations of Papist plots against the King were rife.

Meehan was accused of being a Catholic priest and challenged to make an oath of allegiance and religious supremacy to the King.

Fresh from his studies in Rome, and fired with religious enthusiasm, he refused. His death was worse than mere hanging. In May of 1679 he was sentenced 'to be hanged by the neck and cut down alive and his bowels to be taken out and while he still liveth to be burnt and his head cut off, that his body be divided into four parts and his head and quarters be placed as it should please the Lord King to assign'. In short, Meehan was to be hung, drawn and quartered.

It needed a great deal of skill to ensure that the priest was not only still alive but conscious enough to witness a portion of his own intestine being burned in front of him. As a well-educated man he would have been well aware of the details of his impending death in the square at Ruthin. He had a full three months in which to contemplate his fate. His last statement was published as a broadsheet:

> Now God Almighty is pleased I should suffer martyrdom. His Holy name be praised since I die for my religion. But you have no right to put me to death in this country. However, God forgive you for I do and shall always pray for you especially those that were so good to me in my distress. I pray God bless our King and defend him from his enemies and convert him to the Holy Catholic faith.

Meehan could have avoided his fate by swearing allegiance to the Crown and acknowledging the King as the head of the Church. He chose not to.

Chapter Six

Betrayal, dandruffy coffee and Max Bygraves

I made an early start from Ruthin because I knew that we faced a long ride of almost twenty miles that day. We also had to go back through the Clwydians and that meant there would be a lot of uphill work for the horses. The second half of my route was to coincide with the Offa's Dyke long-distance footpath. It was one of the few sizeable stretches which was marked on the map as being a bridleway. I was looking forward to meeting other travellers and comparing notes with them. The first six or seven miles were along lanes but in those first two hours we met only two cars. At one point the view back across the Vale of Clwyd was so stunning that I just tied the horses up to a fence beside the road to take a picture. That was when the third car of the morning came along.

Later on, we stopped for lunch where the map shows a viewing point. Molly and I viewed while Kate got on with the more important business of eating. After an hour's rest I saddled up and set off again – this time along the section which was on the Offa's Dyke path. I started to meet other travellers – hearty young men for the most part. I did come across an older man travelling with two small white dogs – West Highland terriers, I think. As soon as we stopped to talk the dogs flopped down at his feet and lay there panting. Robert and his dogs had left Chepstow, at the south end of the Dyke, the previous Monday and he hoped to finish at Prestatyn the next day. Ten days to do the whole trip. I had allowed six weeks, and it had taken me

Robert, who was walking the Offa's Dyke path with his two dogs, was under strict instructions to ring home every night to tell his wife how the dogs were doing.

almost one week to do the distance he hoped to travel in the next thirty-six hours. I asked him if he was enjoying the walk, but instead of answering he told me how many miles a day he was averaging and the distance he had covered on his best day. He had also lost six pounds on the trip so far and bought himself a pair of wide braces decorated with American flags. Robert was under instructions to ring his wife each night and tell her how the dogs were doing.

An hour or so later the path went past a youth hostel and ducked in through a large area of forestry. As it wound upwards the path got narrower and narrower. The horses had to walk in single file. It got worse as the trees started closing in. Branches snagged on the packs and I was riding for yards on end with my head bent down low over Molly's neck. Eventually I had to get off. This left me with a real problem because I could not lead both horses from the ground. I considered tying Kate's lead rope to the back of Molly's saddle, but if something startled either horse then I would be in real trouble. I decided to tie Kate's lead rope back around her neck and let her follow at her own speed. She behaved beautifully – better than I had any right to expect from a raw four-year-old mare.

I was just congratulating myself on my brilliance as a judge of horseflesh when the path ahead took a sudden right-hand turn and headed straight up the hill. There in front of me was a long set of wooden steps. I stopped and cursed for a few minutes. I fished out the map. If we turned back we faced a costly detour along main roads and we would certainly not get to Llangollen that night. But it would be a one-way trip up the steps. I might be able to get the horses up there, but bringing them down would be impossible. I tied the horses up and went ahead to assess the size of the task. The steps had been put in to help people walking the Dyke path get up this particularly steep slope. They looked good and strong but would they be tough enough to take the weight of half a tonne of packhorse? The path opened out and levelled off at the top, and I felt sure that if we could get past the steps we would be all right. It's funny how wrong you can be.

I tried to decide which horse to take up first. Molly was more sure-footed but is less trusting of me. Kate would follow me anywhere but I was worried what Molly might do if she were left behind. In the end I decided to leave Kate tied to a tree at the bottom and lead Molly up first.

My nervousness was starting to get through to the horses, so the sooner I got it over and done with the better. Molly is suspicious of new obstacles and likes to take a long look at things before she takes them on. She sniffed suspiciously at the bottom step. She knew what I was proposing but did not like the idea of it at all. I went up the first couple of steps and talked and clucked to her. She put a foot on the first step, decided that it would take her weight, and we were away. She had decided to get the ordeal over and done with as quickly as possible. I had to take the steps two at a time to stay ahead of her and did not have the time to look back to see how she was doing. All I knew was that there was the sound of a snorting horse thundering up close behind me and that she was not going to stop halfway through. She had set the pace and I had to stay ahead or be run over. I was taking a stupid risk. She could drop a hoof down between two of the steps and get her leg trapped, or a plank might break leaving splinters in her hock. When we got to the top, my heart was pounding with the combined exertion and fear and finally triumph. Molly and I stood still for a moment while we got our breath back.

I then tied Molly to a convenient tree and ran back down to where Kate was waiting. She whickered at me as I reappeared. I was fairly confident that she would follow, although her pack worried me because of the steepness of the climb. I was concerned that it might slip backwards or off to one side and this could be dangerous if it happened halfway up. I decided to carry the pack up to the top one piece at a time and then lead Kate up afterwards. I took off the small saddlebags and the tent and carried them back up to the top of the steps where I had left Molly. She did not like being left alone and had wrapped her tether two or three times around the tree. I could really have done with some human help at this time. If only a party of walkers would come along the path I could get one of them to hold Molly while I took care of Kate. No one appeared. I felt terribly alone.

Molly was getting even more agitated and I could not risk leaving her alone for much longer. It would take four or five trips to bring Kate's gear up by hand and Molly was whipping herself up into a real frenzy. Kate would have to come up right then – pack and all. So I

Things were going well until we came around a corner and found these.

rushed down, untied her and led her to the first step. Without so much as breaking her stride, she walked calmly and quietly up the steps, taking them one at a time as though it was part of her daily routine. She walked so slowly and quietly that the pack stayed firmly in place. As Kate and I came into view, there was an exchange of whickers between the horses and Molly stopped treating her tree as a maypole. It occurred to me that the two of them had not been out of each other's sight for at least three months; to be separated under these conditions was not really fair. I felt excluded from the growing relationship between the two horses, and guilty about what I was doing to these peaceful creatures who would much rather be at home in a field than out here with me.

I reloaded the bits of the pack I had carried up by hand, remounted and got under way. I started singing as a way of releasing tension, but within a quarter of a mile the celebratory verses gave way to curses as the trees started to close in again. I was soon forced to get off and walk. Forests can be beautiful, serene places to travel through, but this one was beginning to feel oppressive. Again I let Kate find her own way while I led Molly. At first we made good progress, but within another half mile the ground started to get black and boggy. Boards, chicken wire and timber had been put down to make a sort of walkway – fine for humans but hard on horses. The chicken wire was slippery for their steel-shod feet. The path had just started to traverse a gentle tree-lined slope when, straight ahead of me, over an extremely boggy area where a stream came down off the slope above us, I saw a narrow wooden bridge. Again I tied the horses up while I worked out a strategy for getting around this particular problem. It was actually more an elevated walkway than a bridge – about four feet wide and forty yards long, with a zigzig in the middle. I did not fancy trying to persuade the horses to walk across it: they might slip off the side, or one of the timbers might break, and I could find myself literally miles from anywhere with a horse with a cut leg, or even worse. I walked up and down looking for the driest place to lead the horses across. There didn't seem to be anywhere suitable: the

*The trees closed in
so tightly that I had
to get off and walk.
Kate was left to
follow in her own
time.*

ground looked boggy both up and downstream of the bridge.
Eventually I settled on a spot about fifteen yards upstream from the
walkway. Leaving Kate tied to a tree, I led Molly forwards. She didn't
like the look of it but followed me into the mud anyway. The peaty
goo came up to just above my ankles. When Molly stepped in, her
legs disappeared up to her chest. She rolled her eyes in fear. If I close
my eyes now I can still see that wild-eyed look of betrayal. She froze
for a moment, looked back towards where Kate was standing and
made a huge effort to get back to dry ground. All I could do was to
back away from the flailing hooves and let her get on with it. After
what felt like an age she managed to thrash her way to firm ground.
She walked back to Kate and stood beside her one remaining friend,
shaking and shivering with fear.

Now what the hell could I do? I couldn't go back. I couldn't get the
horses down those bloody steps. I couldn't see a way to go on. The
path between the steps and the bridge had been girded by a solid wall
of trees, and there were no alternative routes marked on the map. I
stood by the horses and stroked their heads and talked as calmly to
them as I could. Even I could hear the quaver in my voice. The sweat
had gone cold on my body. I wished that someone would come along
the footpath.

After a few minutes, Molly's breathing settled back to normal. I felt her pulse. It was still racing – but then so was mine. I re-examined the raised walkway. I jumped up and down on it. It seemed firm enough, but could I persuade the horses to cross it? There seemed to be no alternative but to try.

I untied Molly and led her towards the wooden contraption. She sniffed at it and then backed off. I gave her time. She came forward, even put a foot on it, but she just did not trust me any more. I coaxed and cajoled but she was getting even more distressed.

There was only one more thing to try, and that was to take Kate first. What worried me most was that Molly might still refuse to follow – especially if the crossing went badly with Kate. And Kate might then refuse to make a return trip. I could wind up with a terrified horse on either side of the bridge. Then I really would be in trouble.

I unloaded the pack and ferried it across the walkway in four trips. I procrastinated for a few minutes then started to lead Kate towards the wooden structure. She dealt with the bridge as calmly as she had the steps. At one point her hoof slipped off the edge, but even this failed to unsettle her. We got safely across and I tied her to a tree while I went back for Molly. At least I knew that the bridge was strong enough to take the weight of a horse.

Molly had watched Kate cross safely and must have realised that the only way she was going to get back to her friend was to cross the walkway. She approached it gingerly, took a good sniff at it. She looked up to where Kate was standing and clattered quickly and noisily across. Again there were a few celebratory snorts and whickers as the horses were reunited. I promised myself that I would not use any more bridle paths unless they were recommended by someone who really knew that they were passable. Again I waited for the three of us to calm down before setting off along the path once more.

It then started to open out and ahead of us were three walkers, laughing and joking as they came. They were three strong men in their thirties or forties – just the sort I could have done with a few minutes earlier. I asked them if there were any bridges, board walks or flights of steps on the path ahead. They assured me that it was clear, although it became rather boggy where it crossed some moorland on the other side of the forest.

The three walkers were firemen from Liverpool doing the Offa's Dyke path to raise money to send a local child to America for hospital treatment. They were expecting to complete the trip in eleven days. They asked me if I had seen Robert and his dogs whom they kept on passing along the way.

'It's like the hare and the tortoise,' one of them said. 'Robert just keeps steadily on, while we get waylaid by the pubs. Then we have to walk on fast to catch back up with our schedule.'

They were carrying camping equipment, but had actually spent most of their nights at the various fire-brigade stations along the way. They said how lucky I was not to have to carry a pack and to have a horse to do all the work for me. At that precise moment carrying a 50-lb rucksack did not seem to be that much of a price to pay to avoid all the aggravation I was having. I am sure that the horses would have been happier if I had decided to do the trip the sensible way and carry my own gear.

The horses and I carried on until we came to a gate taking us out of the forest. There was a further two miles of soft peaty going across open, heather-covered moorland. It had been dry and hot for several days and a crust had formed on the surface. In places the horses would break through to the soft mushy peat underneath. I was immensely relieved when we got onto the hard metalled road which took us the remaining seven miles down into Llangollen. I split Kate's pack between the two horses and walked the last five miles because I felt that they had suffered enough that day already.

I started asking people I met at the houses scattered along the side of the road about places to stay. Eventually a group of builders suggested that I should try Mrs Davies who has a paddock where she lets space for campers and caravans. Her field had plenty of grass and she seemed quite happy with the £10 a night I offered. Toilets and coin-in-the-slot showers were also part of the deal. There were a few permanent caravans in the field and a couple of other campers. It seemed like a good place to stay for a day or so. The horses soon settled down to graze while I set up my home and started on supper.

My plastic bag of food was beginning to smell of bad egg so I cleaned all the packets under running water while I had access to a sink. First, though, I had to boil some water for the instant meal of vegetable ragout and dumpling mix. I am afraid it looked much like the pasta mush of the previous night. I have offered my dog more appetising dishes. Out came the curry mix again. I was more careful with the quantities this time, and at least what I was eating had an identifiable flavour.

I had saved a real treat for afters. Some friends had given me a sachet of instant apple and custard mix. It was a foil packet with a most attractive girl lying half in, half out of her tent, while consuming her supper of 'Raven Foods Outdoor Cuisine' straight from the packet. The instructions told me to add boiling water and leave for five minutes. I had not anticipated that the foil sachet would get so hot and suffered a painful period while I contrived a place to stand the sachet where it would not fall over. Another time I would make it in a mug. It tasted absolutely delicious, real nursery comfort food – just what I needed at the end of a difficult day.

Coffee completed the meal, although I couldn't understand why the powdered milk would not dissolve properly. There were white specks floating on the surface of the liquid and collecting as a sludge in the bottom of the mug. I tried fishing them out with a spoon but soon gave that up as a bad job. I went ahead and sipped the coffee trying, with only limited success, to strain the bits out with my lips. Halfway through, I realised that my mug had been packed beside the horse brush. Horse dandruff has a flavour and texture all of its own.

I finished the day with one of Mrs Davies's spurty ten-pence-in-the-slot showers, getting the temperature perfect just as the money ran out. I rinsed the soap off with cold water before crawling gratefully into my sleeping bag. It was another cold night. It was at 3.30 a.m., when my fellow campers played the second Max Bygraves record of the night, that I resolved to buy myself a new sleeping bag.

Chapter Seven

Pretentious blue stockings, a tough birth and a stubborn widow

I slept through the dawn chorus, only to have Kate wake me up just before six o'clock by snorting and stamping her feet beside the tent. I pulled the sleeping bag over my head, but she persisted with a modest whinny. I tried to ignore her. She started threatening the structural integrity of the tent by pawing at the pegs. I conceded defeat and got up to give both horses their food, before staggering back to bed to listen to my colleagues on *Farming Today* tell the nation's early-rising élite why they should think twice before eating a beefburger. The sound of the horses munching their pony nuts gave way to the sound of rough equine tongues licking plastic bowls clean of every last fragment of feed. After the ritual inspection of each other's empty bowls, the horses walked off to find more grass.

I decided that both they and I deserved a day off so I lay there and dozed until the rumblings of my own stomach drove me out of bed. When I went down to wash and shave, Mrs Davies was busy bumbling about her slightly scruffy farmyard. It was home to a rich variety of stock including a small herd of cattle, chickens, numerous cats, two pigs, five dogs and a couple of Muscovy ducks doing what comes naturally to them. They had somehow managed to embroil a chicken in their bizarre and frenzied sexual activities.

Mrs Davies was hefting a terribly heavy-looking bale of hay across to her cattle. She was a small, grey-haired woman, of an age when she should have been thinking about bus passes and crochet rather than feeding livestock. We had a brief chat, during which I told her about my trip and she told me about the pleasures and pains of running a sixty-acre farm by herself. I offered to help her with her bales, but she said that she only had two more to do. She said it in a way that made it clear that she had done all the others without my help and she did not want to be deprived of the satisfaction of finishing the job herself.

As I walked into town I stopped at the tourist information centre and picked up some leaflets about Llangollen. I sat in a café enjoying a long, slow, greasy breakfast while deciding what to do with my day off. An hour later, decisions made and stomach full, I headed out of town towards an extraordinary house called Plas Newydd – or, in English, the New Place. It is about a mile out of town and is now a tourist attraction. In fact, it has been attracting a stream of visitors ever since two bizarre women moved in just over two hundred years ago. The two of them would have hated the idea of their house being filled with gawking, common people. They preferred to attract gawking aristocrats.

At first sight, the house looks like an Elizabethan timber-frame manor with its contrasting black and white exterior. The area in front is covered in box hedges and shrubs which have been clipped and shaped into an odd collection of topiary sculptures. The effect is of a giant Dali-esque chess game being played out on the front lawn. As I came closer to the building I dropped the idea that it was Elizabethan. What I had taken to be beams turned out to be intricately carved

Mrs Davies, who still runs a sixty-acre farm at the age of 76.

columns, arches and even Greek urn shapes superimposed on the white painted walls of the house. The house has three large porches and heavily leaded bay windows. The excessive detail and general over-twiddlyness of it all fools the eye into believing that the house is much larger than it really is. In fact, Plas Newydd is nothing more than a decent-sized farmhouse with ideas way above its station. And that is exactly what its former occupants had intended.

Plas Newydd used to be the home of an eccentric pair of English aristocrats called Sarah Ponsonby and Eleanor Butler. They met at boarding school in Kilkenny where they forged a friendship that lasted for half a century. Their families became aware of their passionate liaison and, with indecent haste, decided to marry one of the girls off and send the other to a convent. The two girls could not bear the idea of being parted, so they eloped – if that is the right word for their particular circumstances. Their first attempt to escape ended in them being picked up at Waterford in southern Ireland. Both were dressed in men's clothing, and Sarah, the younger of the two, was armed with a pistol. They were brought to heel, but again escaped. It eventually dawned on the families that their attempts to force the two women to conform were stirring up even more scandal than letting them have their own way.

Free, but relatively penniless, the two of them eventually settled in Llangollen – a modest little town by the bridge over the River Dee. At that time, anyone travelling from London to Ireland would be sure to pass through Llangollen and there was a steady flow of aristocratic travellers between the two countries. Setting up home there was a bit like running away to the Watford Gap services on the M1 in search of peace and quiet. If they really wanted to drop out of society, Llangollen was an odd place to choose.

Eleanor and Sarah lived, and held court, at Plas Newydd for half a century. They kept exhaustive, not to say exhausting, diaries detailing the great events and the tiny minutiae of their lives with equal diligence. Unfortunately, as the ladies grew older their grasp of the distinction between the relevant and the irrelevant became ever more tenuous. Minutiae would loom large in their lives; wars or social deprivation rated merely a line or two. Their house became a gossip exchange for all the fascinating tittle-tattle of aristocratic life. Nobody who was anybody would have dared to pass their way without dropping in and paying their respects; who knows what rumours might be circulated about those who failed to pay homage to the two Ladies of Llangollen. Everyone from the monarch downwards (but not too far downwards) came to visit them. And there was a terrible dilemma for those who were not quite of the highest rank – the borderline aristocrats. Not to offer to call might offend Eleanor and Sarah, and such a snub would immediately be followed by some deliciously malicious gossip being spread around select circles on both sides of the Irish Sea. But offers to call from people whom the two ladies considered to be beneath them might result in a curt, rather insulting response and even more poisonous gossip being spread around.

I was not disappointed by the inside of their house. It is hideously over-decorated and over-ornate. It must have been a terrible place to dust in the days when open coal fires were the only form of heating. No wonder they sacked so many servants. The plethora of carved oak, both inside and outside the house, stemmed from the two ladies' insistence that visitors and guests brought them some piece of carved oak or stained glass. The inside has the feel of a miniature Tudor mansion, with wood panelling everywhere. Churches and temples from all over the world were plundered to decorate this

The most pretentious farmhouse in the country – designed and developed by two eighteenth-century lesbians.

The Vale of Llangollen.

place just so that the aristocracy of eighteenth-century Britain could have a meal and a gossip. The modest house was really only a cottage with a few rooms, but the ladies would have been terribly insulted if any of their guests had referred to it as such. Sarah and Eleanor did their best to make use of their scant residential resources. The house had a library, State Room and State Bedchamber where the two women spent their nights in a massive four-poster bed. Newspapers of the time referred to the 'two Irish ladies who have settled in so romantic a manner in Denbighshire'. Many of their own diary entries finish with the loaded phrases that they spent the evening in 'delicious retirement' or 'exquisite retirement'.

Plas Newydd now attracts tens of thousands of visitors each year and has become a place of pilgrimage for lesbians from all over the world. The visitors' book makes fascinating reading. There, alongside Ed and Candice from Saskatoon, Canada, were the names of Gwendoline and Wendy, Chrissie and Tatts, Amanda and Sue, and comments such as 'Right on, sisters' and 'Brave place, brave women'.

I spent the rest of the day in Llangollen and managed to buy a new sleeping bag. When I got back to the tent, I made some tea and fell asleep before drinking it. I woke to the sound of Mrs Davies calling me to come down and give her some help. I must have mentioned that I had worked with cows and she wanted me to give her a hand with one of her heifers which was having a difficult time giving birth to its first calf. In my rush to get out of the tent, I spilt my undrunk tea on my virgin sleeping bag. When I got down to the byre the cow had already started calving. Two tiny pink hooves were just starting to stick out of her back end. I washed my arms, James Herriot style, and checked to make sure that the calf was presenting correctly. Sometimes calves will come with their head bent right back. Then you have a real Herculean struggle on your hands, trying to push the youngster back in to rearrange it while the poor old cow is still doing her level best to push it out. Fortunately I was spared this. When I pushed my hand in along the legs, I was able to feel a warm, slimy nose. It was just a big calf trying to get out of a small cow. I had suspected that this would be the case. Earlier on in the day I had noticed Mrs Davies's big Charollais bull. The meat trade likes Charollais because they produce large lean carcasses in the finished animal. The trouble is that calves from the Continental bulls often have wide shoulders and hips and that can make giving birth a tough affair – especially for young heifers like this one. All this is rather hard on cattle – some people say it is cruel. However, it is no worse than the biological miseries people inflict upon themselves when a small woman marries a large man.

With Mrs Davies's heifer it should have been pretty simple – merely a well-timed and well-directed pull. The heifer had made life difficult for us by climbing into a narrow feeding area at one end of the byre. She was lying down and had got one leg trapped under the feed barrier. Stuck like that I could not pull in the right direction. We had to hacksaw through the barrier to release the heifer. There was some urgency because cattle lose their strength pretty quickly once they have started contracting. It took me about ten minutes to remove the barrier, but by then the heifer was too exhausted to stand up. However, even with her lying down, I was able to get the right angle and she was still contracting. I tied two short lengths of rope around the protruding feet and, after three more tug-assisted contractions, the calf slipped out into the world. It was a big one. I pushed my finger into its mouth to make sure that its airway was clear, rubbed the worst of the yeuch off with a twist of straw and put it down by the heifer's head. She gave one of those long, contented maternal lows and started licking.

There is always something magical about a birth – even if it is an animal which is likely to wind up sharing a plate with a handful of chips in a Berni Steak Inn. I felt pretty pleased with myself, and Mrs Davies felt pretty pleased with me. She not only offered me a celebratory sherry, but she also let me off that night's rent. I cleaned up, and we retreated to her kitchen table leaving the calf and the young mother to get on with it.

Under the influence of the sherry and the successful calving Mrs Davies opened up a bit and started talking about her life. She had moved to the farm in the mid-fifties with her husband, Ben. They had built the business up to include all the stock and the caravan and camping business. Ben died in May 1979, just six weeks before his sixty-fifth birthday. There were no children.

I asked her why she kept going. She could have sold the farm for a lot of money – £250000 at least. Or she could rent out the land and just keep the house.

'Because I'm stubborn,' she said. 'I'll keep going as long as I can manage.' I asked her why she felt the need to keep going, but she could not provide an answer which satisfied either of us. She just felt it was somehow the right thing to do. It was as though by giving up she would be betraying Ben in some way.

Throughout our conversation Mrs Davies kept on saying 'we' when talking about her plans for the farm and what would be happening. I asked her why. She said that it was just a habit left over from when it had been her and Ben. I then realised why she was refusing to let the farm go. She would have had to let go of Ben as well, to have reburied his presence, his memory, along with his body, and she was not ready for that yet. She probably never would be.

Chapter Eight

Bilingual football, Mr Magoo and too many horses

The next morning Kate would not eat her food and I was not happy about it. A sick horse was the last thing I needed. I carefully checked her over, felt over her body for any signs of illness, smelt her breath, had a good listen at her side and was pleased to hear a few gurgles. Horses have a long and active set of intestines. If a horse is gurgling and farting, that is a sure sign that she is in good condition. I sat and watched her while I had my breakfast. She seemed bright and alert, but still off her food. By ten past six I had packed up and was listening to my colleagues on *Farming Today* telling people why they should not eat eggs. I lingered over my cup of tea so as to give Molly enough time for her breakfast to settle down.

At 6.30 I led the horses through Mrs Davies's yard. She was already up and about, lugging bales around and talking, singing and cursing at her stock. She seemed genuinely sad to see me go. She had several more cattle due to calve in the coming weeks. I am sure that the two were not connected. I wondered to myself how much longer she would be able to keep running the farm. I did not like the idea of her having to give up her independence. Even though I hardly knew her, I felt in some way as though I was walking out on her.

I said goodbye and even gave her a peck on her wrinkled cheek and a quick hug. I mounted Molly and we set off through the quiet streets of Llangollen. The bridge over the canal was a bit steep and the horses' metal shoes slipped on the road as we came down the other side. At the top of the high street the traffic lights were against us. I felt self-conscious as we waited for them to change. Kate did a dump. It increased my embarrassment but I was pleased to see that it came out as a greenish pile of discrete nuggets. At least it was pretty normal. Our route took us up past Plas Newydd and then along a track with a sign saying 'Unfit for motor vehicles'. It was rocky, steep, hard going. I got off Molly and transferred some of the bags from Kate to Molly, allowing Kate to follow at her own pace. She stopped for a breather a couple of times on the way up. I was glad to see that she was picking at the bushes on the way. At one point she started chewing at the soil. I did not know whether that was a good or a bad sign.

The track joined a tarmac lane and then, within a mile, we were dropping down into the valley of the River Ceiriog. The map had two little chevrons marked across the road, indicating that it was a steep hill. It was terribly steep. I dismounted and walked between the horses. Three abreast like that, we took up most of the width of the road. I have never taken one horse down such a steep hill, let alone two. The horses hated it as their steel-shod feet slipped and slid and skidded on the metalled road. The lane finally levelled out and joined the road which leads the eight or nine miles up to Llanarmon at the top of the valley.

It was still only ten o'clock and we had made good time. Progress was so good that I had stopped worrying about Kate and started enjoying the ride. We eventually halted for a break at a small bridge over the river. It left a comfortable four miles to do in the afternoon. As I waited for the kettle to boil I watched the horses standing in the sun, their tails flicking laconically at the odd fly. The bright light glistened on their coats where it flowed over their newly-developed muscles. I felt proud of them. I could not believe my good fortune to have found a job where I got paid to do this.

An hour or so later we had all had a quick zizz and even Kate was ready to be on her way, so I saddled up and we made a start on the last four miles to Llanarmon. Up ahead of us I could see a man trimming

There was a growing bond between the two horses – one from which I felt excluded.

a hedge. He had white hair which suggested he was quite old, but he was attacking the hedge with such vigour that he could not be as old as I had taken him for. Hearing the sound of the horses' feet on the road, he looked up, put down his saw and straightened up to watch our approach. Not to have stopped to talk would have been a terrible insult.

'Lovely horses,' he said, knowing the best way to open a conversation. Mentioning the lovely weather would have been superfluous, asking where I was going might have seemed too nosy.

It is bad etiquette to stay sitting imperiously on a horse while someone on foot talks up at you, so I got off.

'Like them then, do you?' said I, fishing for more compliments. It was still a novelty having people admiring the horses. It is a double delight because you are being complimented on your good sense for buying them and on your skill in keeping them looking good. I wanted to hear more.

'They're lovely. Good. Strong,' he said in a sort of conversational shorthand. He walked around Molly, felt her legs, her strong neck. 'Suffolk in her, I reckon.' Then on to Kate. The inspection was slightly longer, slightly more thorough. 'Can I buy the foal, then?' – the ultimate compliment – came as a bit of a shock. Despite Kate's sudden change in behaviour I had convinced myself that she was just a little off colour.

'How long do you think before she drops it, then?' I asked, in the hope that it would sound as though I knew she was in foal but was just testing him. Emyr Lloyd plays the part of the joking local, but I don't think he is a man who is easily fooled. He said he thought it would be between one and two months before anything happened. That was cutting it a bit fine for finishing the trip.

Emyr seemed in no rush to get on with his hedge. His wife must have been used to such extended conversations, for she soon came out bearing cups of tea for both of us. I could see that this might be a long one, so I slackened the girths and tied the horses to a nearby gate. Emyr said that he particularly liked Kate because of her Clydesdale blood. His father used to keep them – full-sized ones, not crossbreeds like her. He described her as a half-leg pony. She was the pre-war equivalent of a pick-up truck – a general-purpose animal used for personal transport, light haulage around the farm, even a bit of harrowing. At hay time the half-leg would be hitched up in front of the real heavy horses just to add a bit of extra power.

I asked him if I should stop working Kate if he was so sure she was in foal. He said that would do more harm than good. 'She's in work now, keep her at it. We used to work them right up until the last day, let the mare out of the shafts and she would drop it that night.'

And what about afterwards, what then?

'Nothing. Just give her a day off and get going again with the foal at heel. It'll be lovely.' Lovely was Emyr's favourite word.

I asked him about the farmers and what they did for stallions for their mares. He told me that sometimes they used to take their mares to a local farm where they had a farm stallion. 'He was a working stallion. We would take the mare over there. He might be working with a plough up on top somewhere. When he saw us coming, smelled us coming more like, the owner had to unharness him. Let him go. He'd come chargin' down the field to do his job. Have her there and then. Lovely. Better stand out the way, mind.

'Then there was the Association stallion. Better bred. Had to pay more for that. A man used to come around with him. Rode a pony leading the stallion. Would visit farms to do his job. No one trusted the man though. Wouldn't let him in the house with the womenfolk. Lovely. Good job!'

Half an hour later I extricated myself from Emyr's wonderful company and we were under way once again, making good time down the road to Llanarmon. I was actually taking quite a large diversion into Wales and would be leaving the border ten or eleven miles behind to the east.

Llanarmon, which sits in the flat valley bottom surrounded by trees, turned out to be as pretty as I had been told it was. It has a couple of dozen houses, a good big church and two nice pubs – just the right ratio. I tied the horses up under a tree and went into one of the pubs to ask about finding somewhere to stay. The lady behind the bar said that she would go and ring someone. Within seconds she was back with instructions for me to continue up the lane to a farm called Sarffle where Emyr Owens would offer the horses a field for the night. Emyr was obviously a common name in the area.

By three o'clock that afternoon the horses were happily grazing in a lovely field with the river wandering through it, I had the tent pitched and the Lilo inflated. A pretty good day all round.

I went up to the farm to get some water. Emyr Owens was in the yard standing beside the open door of his car, singing at the top of his beautiful tenor voice. When he saw me, he stopped and explained that he was trying to learn a new song which he was playing on the cassette in the car.

We talked farming for a bit and I learnt that Emyr is about my age. He had taken on the farm and set about improving the land and trying to make the holding pay its way. I have no idea about the state of his overdraft but the signs were everywhere that he was a first-rate farmer. His fields were lush and green and a good three weeks ahead of his neighbour's in the growth of grass. His sheep looked healthy, no coughing and no trace of the dreaded foot rot. He had managed to improve the productivity without damaging the natural beauty of the place. That is the trouble with being a farmer: the standard of your work is there for everyone with an eye to see.

After talking farming we moved on to other things. Emyr said that he was going to a football match that evening, and offered to take me along. It was the final of a local league between the two top teams, one from each side of the border. I hate football. It bores me sideways, but after the match we were going to call in at the pub. The football was as boring as I feared it would be, although it was odd hearing the Welsh-language equivalents of 'On the head', 'Over here', and 'Bloody hell, ref'. Emyr told me that the referee did not speak Welsh and he was oblivious to the stream of obscenities aimed at him during the match.

On the way home, Emyr and I called in at the pub five miles down the valley from Llanarmon. We soon became embroiled in an extensive drinking session with a number of the locals. I seem to remember buying and consuming quite a few drinks. We left and moved on to one of the pubs in the village. One thing led to another, and I had a few more drinks. I do not seem to remember whether I bought them or someone else did. I know that I have to stop at two and a half pints otherwise I get a terrible punishment in the morning. I thought I had four pints. Emyr says that he stopped counting at six.

It was well after midnight by the time I got back to the field and I had a tough time remembering where I had pitched the tent. After fifteen minutes blundering around in the dark I managed to find it in the next field along and crawled gratefully inside. I lay down and heard a gentle shushing noise. I wondered what it could be as I sank down . . . onto the hard ground. I had knocked the plug out of the Lilo. I bent down to blow it up again. It was not a pleasant experience. I persevered manfully, but I should have put up with the hard ground. When I eventually got around to lying down, I felt very bad – very bad indeed. I spent the next hour sitting inside the tent propped against the saddles waiting for the ground to settle down. It took a long time. By about two in the morning it felt solid enough to let me lie down. I had to get up several times in the night for entirely natural purposes. The field by the river was quite rocky. Emyr had decided to leave it unimproved so as to maintain its rich flora. The rich flora included quite a few thistles. One way or another, it was not a good night's sleep.

I don't remember it being a particularly cold night, but when I woke up there was ice on the outside of the tent. But it was a bright sunny morning. An awfully bright sunny morning. The sort of day which makes you glad to be alive – unless you have some pretty good reasons for wanting to be dead. I had at least six pints of reasons. As I stood there getting rid of some of them I looked around for the horses. They were down by the river about a hundred yards away. I was not wearing my glasses and they looked like three lumps. *Three* lumps? Kate was paying a lot of attention to a small blurred lump on the ground. At first I thought it was a sheep. Wearing only my underpants I picked my way towards the horses, trying to avoid Emyr's thistles and rocks as I went. I must have looked rather odd, almost naked, treading carefully and squinting forwards like Mr Magoo. It took me a long time to work out what had happened. My brain never works at maximum efficiency first thing in the morning anyway. It was also getting poor information fed to it by my badly focused eyes, and then there was the remains of the alcohol which was still coursing through my veins. My head was pounding. I think that I wanted to believe that it was a sheep that Kate was licking so tenderly. I must have been within twenty yards of them before I had to acknowledge that it was a foal. A part of me still clutched at the hope that it was someone else's foal which had got in with my horses, but the rest of my brain was busy recognising that the foal was wet and obviously fresh to the world.

I am quite proud of what I did next. I ran away . . . back to the tent as fast as I could go. I ignored the thistles and the rocks, threw on a tee-shirt and jeans, found my glasses, picked up the camera and switched on the tape recorder. Fifteen years of being a journalist had paid off, and my first instinct was to start recording what was happening. Kate Adie would have been proud of me. I wince when I play it back to hear the sentimental sobs and declarations of 'She's done it' as I ran back towards the horses.

Kate had made a serious start on licking the foal dry. As I approached she gave off one of those quintessentially maternal whickers which welled up from the back of her throat. It was an expression of her own contentment and a reassurance to the foal which was lying on the ground looking dazed. It was mouse-coloured with tiny brown hooves, four white socks and a perfectly symmetrical white blaze in the middle of its forehead. It was skinny with unbelievably long legs – far too long to fit inside Kate's belly.

I kept my distance and walked over to pat Molly, although I really wanted to pat the foal and congratulate Kate. It was a truly wonderful moment in that quiet Welsh field on a clear spring morning. I was experiencing a terrible jumble of emotions: I was proud of Kate for behaving so well and for coping with this difficult event; I was relieved and grateful that the foal had come safely into the world; I felt guilty about what I had put her through and the risks I had taken with her and her baby's life. And then there was the effect of my once-in-a-decade hangover.

During my emotional crisis Kate continued to tend to her foal. After a few minutes she began nudging it to its feet. As the sun dried its coat, the foal started turning from slick black wetness to mouse-grey softness. After half a dozen attempts the foal was wobbling unsteadily on its incredibly long legs. It was even more difficult to see how all that length could have folded up inside Kate's womb. I reckon that I must have come on the scene within five minutes of the

It was difficult to believe that all this foal could have been tucked up inside Kate.

foal actually being born. Within another fifteen minutes it was nosing ineffectually around Kate's teats. I approached Kate on the opposite side to the foal and quickly checked to see if she had any milk. She seemed to have plenty. I guided the foal's mouth home to the teat. As it suckled, its tiny tail flicked from side to side. It was a filly. I retreated to the tent to put the kettle on, get properly dressed and take some aspirin. Actually, I did that lot in reverse order.

As the kettle was boiling I filled up the horses' bowls – Kate's received a few extra handfuls of nuts. And then a few more. I took the feed, my tea and a packet of fig rolls over to the horses. Under normal circumstances Kate would have come rushing over as soon as she saw me approaching with her bowl. This time she stayed put, with her foal sitting on the ground with a slightly bemused look on her face. Molly stood beside them looking proud and protective. This was ridiculous – I was starting to get sentimental again and imagining emotions for the animals which were not really there. Molly came trotting over towards me, but only got halfway before suddenly stopping, looking around at Kate and the foal and then trotting back to stand beside them again. I put the bowls down in front of the horses and went to sit on a small hummock to drink my tea and ruminate over my fig rolls and my predicament.

As I sat on my little tump eating my fig rolls, drinking my tea, pulling tiny bits of thistle out of my feet and wondering when the aspirins would start making me feel better, I worked out Kate's life history: born in Ireland in 1986 where she spent the first three years of her life running more or less wild, sent across to Wales in a ship, broken to the bit and the saddle before being sold at Lampeter horse sale, spent the winter in Wales, bought by the BBC, taken to Buckinghamshire where she was fitted with a pack saddle and trained to be led from another horse, then back to Wales again, where she walked fifteen miles a day and was turned out in a different field every night for two weeks only to choose this spot as the place to drop her foal. If that's not a life of exploitation, I don't know what is.

For all that, she looked contented and healthy and had produced a good strong foal at the end of it all. Thank God.

I was full of remorse about using Kate as a packhorse during her pregnancy.

Chapter Nine

Dyke diggers, Allegro drivers and British Rail

The birth of the foal left me with some major logistical problems. Emyr told me that, in his father's day, they would have put the mare back into harness within a day or so. The foal would have scampered along beside its mother as she worked in the fields. I could have continued the trip with the foal running along beside Kate, but there was a good chance that she would have scampered into the path of an oncoming articulated lorry.

One way or another, the foal and Kate would have to stay together – and that meant that she could not finish the trip. I could try to sell both of them and buy myself another horse, but it had taken me nearly three months to find Kate and Molly. The thought of trying to buy another horse, which might not get on with Molly or might be unsound, was too much to contemplate. I would never finish the trip in time. I decided that the only option was to get Kate home to the field behind my house in Buckinghamshire and continue the trip on foot using Molly as a packhorse. There were another 150 miles between Llanarmon and the Severn Bridge – so much for my gentleman's ride through the countryside of the borders.

The next problem was to find out how soon the foal would be able to take the four-hour road journey to Buckinghamshire. I decided that I needed an expert and Emyr Lloyd, the man who had been cutting down hedges, was the closest I had come to one. He had been right about Kate being in foal even though he was wrong about the timing. I saddled up Molly and set off down the valley to find him.

Riding was an unpleasant experience. I am told that when you have a hangover your main problem is dehydration. When a body loses a lot of water its cells shrink a little bit – they lose their turgidity and become flaccid and wrinkled, like a week-old balloon. Most brains are designed to be a pretty tight fit in their skull. Sadly, when brains become dehydrated a certain amount of slop enters the system. I suppose that I could have phoned Emyr up to ask him what I should do, but somehow the pace of the whole journey through the borders was taking over. A two-hour round trip just to ask someone a few questions did not seem excessive. By the time I got to Emyr's farm my headache had gone and I was feeling much better.

Emyr Lloyd laughed loud and long when I told him what had happened. He laughed at himself for getting the timing wrong, he laughed at me for having to walk the rest of the journey, but most of all he just laughed because he enjoyed the surprises life throws up. He told me that within four days the foal would be fit to travel in a horsebox. He suggested that I try and drive it myself. A delivery driver would tend to go too fast and throw the foal around in the back.

An hour later, and that much wiser about the care of foals and mares, I pointed Molly back up the valley. She seemed to know that she was heading back towards Kate and the foal and it took much less than an hour to get back. As we came down the lane towards the field, Molly let out a long whinny which produced an almost immediate response from Kate. She came trotting up to the gate to greet us with the foal following close at her side. It was less than six hours old and already trotting around. The reunion between the two mares was really quite touching, with lots of low whickers and sniffing. I would have to use the coming four days to get them accustomed to the idea of being apart. I needed to take Molly out on trips by herself.

I spent the afternoon sitting in front of the tent watching the foal cautiously exploring its new world. It never strayed more than a few yards away from Kate and Molly, but it tried to investigate everything within that safe circle. The stream came in for particular scrutiny, as did the tent when I called the horses over for an extra feed. Later on I walked down to the village to ring my wife and tell her what had happened, and to get her to try to find somewhere that I could hire a horsebox. Once back in the field, I set about rationalising my kit. I reckoned that I had to jettison about a quarter of it. The trouble was that Molly had also been carrying two sizeable bags and a roll of gear across the back of my saddle. All this carrying capacity would be lost now that Molly was to become the packhorse.

I looked at the gear spread out on the grass and shuffled it around for a couple of hours. The spare tape recorder had to go, and a few books. Then I had to start cheese-paring. Out went some of my clothes, gone would be the luxury of two sweat shirts, cut six pairs of underpants down to four, ditto socks, drop one pair of trousers. Then it was goodbye radio, goodbye half-bottle of Scotch and – saddest of all – goodbye mouth organ. The decision about whether I

Separating the horses was not going to be easy.

was to become a tea or a coffee drinker over the coming weeks also had to be made. I settled for tea. I would also have to get shot of the riding boots and buy some decent trainers. Decisions made, I settled down to listen to the last but one instalment of *The Archers* I would be hearing for a month or more. I decided that I would have to make room for the radio: Shula was pregnant. Soon after that, I was asleep.

Kate woke me at 5.45 demanding breakfast. I have never been so happy about being woken up before. I fed the horses and got back into bed to listen to my colleagues on *Farming Today* giving their listeners several good reasons for not eating veal. Once the *Today* programme had started on the news for the second time I decided that I should take Molly on a longish ride to get her used to being without Kate. I also wanted to keep her fit. I looked at the map to see if there was anything worth a visit, and I remembered being told about an archaeological dig which was being carried out on a section of Offa's Dyke near to Chirk. I have always had a soft spot for archaeologists – even tried to have an affair with one when I was at college. It did not work out well. She wanted to spend her weekends on her knees down holes.

The dig was taking place on a section of the dyke near a pub. The landlord gave me some fairly hazy instructions about where to find it: I had to walk along a track where there would be a path off to the right leading down through a wood and over a stream. The archaeologists would be working on the opposite side of the stream. 'You can't miss it,' he said. It's strange how often I manage to miss something which I have been assured that 'I can't miss'. The phrase always has the ring of disaster to it.

After missing the unmissable path I took the wrong one, failed to find a bridge across the stream, tried jumping it, almost succeeded and then carried on up the slope where I could hear the buzzing of voices and clinking of tools.

I came out into a clearing to see a group of twenty people lugging buckets of soil around, disagreeing with each other over theodolite readings and scraping away at a small trench cut into a modest earth embankment. Actually, only half of them were looking busy. A major part of archaeology appeared to involve leaning on shovels and drinking tea. The two shovel-leaners closest to me were deep in conversation about the merits of different types of painkiller. None of them were ready for Zimmer frames – at least not yet – but most of them were old enough to be hesitant about the correct way to pronounce Nike.

I was just taking in the scene when a big man of about forty-five, clean-shaven and wearing glasses, invited them to stop 'doing whatever it is you are doing and come over to the trench'. The tea-drinking shovel-leaners moved their shovels closer and carried on drinking and leaning. The lady who had been lugging buckets of soil around put down her twin burdens and sank down to the ground with a big sigh and an audible crackle from her knees. The people stood around the trench in a semicircle. He asked the shovel-leaners to hush a little.

He stood in the trench, demanded that someone hand him a trowel and spoke to his troops. Most college lecturers like to deliver their addresses from a position of advantage – a podium lends authority to a speaker. With archaeology, the hole in the ground is the focal point. Archaeologists look down on people they look up to. All eyes were focused on the man as he started his discourse.

'Now, just to recap for those whose minds have been on other things,' he glanced at the shovel-leaners who looked only slightly sheepish, 'we are trying to establish whether this bank is man-made. If so, is it Mercian, or is it merely spoil tipped from the construction of the railway line which once ran through here?' I was beginning to wonder whether he had noticed me listening in on his lecture. Perhaps this recapping was for my benefit.

'We have only twenty-four hours left before we need to close the excavation up and be away. So we need a dedicated and experienced team. And we don't have that . . .' He left a pause for the moan, the comments and the resultant laughter. The diggers were told what they should be looking for, and the lecture ended with a complimentary comment about the good work being done by Trudi, Stewart and Mary Rose with their theodolite and sighting sticks. Surveying was obviously the most unpopular task, but the lecturer took the opportunity to highlight the importance of knowing precisely where the digging is going on. Trudi, Stewart and Mary Rose basked in their leader's praise.

After the lecture was over the leader took himself off to sit under a tree fifty yards away. The archaeologists returned to their jobs, their enthusiasm rekindled. At least half of the shovel-leaners transformed themselves into participants. I sat down beside Molly, the woman who was keeping the records, and asked her what they were looking for.

'A turf line, which would prove that this was part of Wat's Dyke,' she said. 'The trouble is that the trees and the badgers and the wildlife have so disrupted the bank that it is difficult to know what we have found.'

Quite a conversation developed between the few people working in the trench just in front of us. They were an obviously middle-class group, except for one of them, who was a retired fireman.

'You know you have arrived as an archaeologist when you get thrown out of a hotel for looking like a navvy,' he said. The titter rippled around the women again – partly because of the joke, partly out of a sense of excitement that they too might one day be thrown out of a hotel. It seemed an unlikely concept – about as likely as nuns being done for disorderly behaviour and making an affray. Even with their ever-so-slightly-tatty pullovers and slacks with grubby knees, they could never be mistaken for anything but middle-class ladies.

I asked them if they resented the fact that their leader, who was called David Hill, was sleeping under a tree while they were working so hard. There was not an ounce of displeasure. Molly told me, with a genteel snigger, that the good Dr Hill was not asleep, he was thinking. I left the group in the trench, aware that I was distracting them from their work. Not a hard job – they seemed ready to be distracted at the slightest excuse.

Dr David Hill was in the habit of resting his brain and his body under a tree while his army of amateurs grafted away in the distance.

I went over to David Hill, who had his eyes closed and was giving a pretty good impression of someone asleep under a tree. He heard me approaching and opened one eye. I explained who I was and asked if he could spare me a few minutes.

'Nice people you have on your courses,' I said, as I sat down opposite him.

'They have to be,' he replied. 'If they are not, they leave. This lot are the cream. They have got no safe structure to hang on to. Some people come on our courses for one night a week for twenty weeks a year. They think they are studying archaeology. We tell them nice stories about the way people used to live in the past. Safe warm certainties dished out in safe warm classrooms. There are no certainties for this lot,' he said, gesturing towards his people. 'We may spend days digging this lump and end up showing that it is merely a spoil tip used by the Irish navvies building the railway back there. Any moment now, one of them may turn up a bit of a clay pipe and we'll know that we have all been wasting our time. Except, of course, it won't have been a waste of time. I will then have to con-vince them that it wasn't, so that we can go and dig elsewhere. And that's why they are the best. Better than professionals. Professionals would never dig somewhere just on the off-chance of finding something. Or to prove that it was not important, come to that.'

On my trip I had been thinking about Offa's Dyke and the gargantuan job of defending a wall 200 miles long. There were no minefields to help, no tripwires, no searchlights. Just raw manpower, and there was not much of that around in the year 800.

'Ah, you are suffering from Kipling,' said David Hill. 'The Kiplingesque image of a line of short-skirted Romans standing shoulder to shoulder along Hadrian's Wall looking out to enemy territory. It is all terribly wrong.

'Come with me,' he said, getting carefully to his feet. He led me back up the hill a little to a place where the side of the valley was at its steepest. There was a small earth platform jutting out into the crest of the valley. It could have been man-made, it could have been natural. If it had not been for the trees the view across into Wales would have been magnificent. I said so. He told me to imagine that the trees were not there. It was not an easy thing to do because there were an awful lot of trees to imagine out of existence.

'A place like this would have been manned twenty-four hours a day. If the lookout saw any sort of threat in the valley below he would raise the alarm with a shout or with a horn or with a fire. Runners would be sent from the nearest settlements to further ones. Within a very few minutes a large body of men could be assembled – perhaps not quickly enough to prevent the raiders from coming across the dyke, but soon enough to make sure that they did not have much time to do any damage. The reserves would have been called up in time to stop the raiding party on the way home with their booty.'

But such a system would demand a sophisticated, well-structured society. How could they ensure that a man would be provided to stand watch? He would need to be released from his other work, he would need to be fed and watered.

'They were certainly more civilised and well-structured than Manchester on a Saturday night,' said David Hill. 'As for manpower, Offa's administrators would have calculated that they needed a full-time staff of, say, forty to man the dyke between here and Oswestry. To achieve this, every man in the county would need to spend two weeks, once every three years, on dyke duty. That requirement would be divided up between the hundreds (a group of villages lumped together for administrative purposes), who would, in turn, tell the villages to deliver so many men to a specified place at a specified time. They would have to bring their own food, tools for dyke maintenance, and probably their own weapons. It would then be up to the village to decide how to fulfil such an obligation.'

I began to dream about how exciting parish council meetings of today would be if we were meeting to decide who to send away and for how long to send them. I could nominate a couple of people in my own village I would like to send away for a few months. There is that bloke who cleans his Allegro at 7.30 on a Saturday morning with Chiltern Radio turned up loud. On Sundays at 7.30 in the morning he cuts his lawn. I would like to see him spend a few weeks each summer on lookout duty on Offa's Dyke.

'The dyke was also a marker and a livestock barrier. Any party which got across could not fail to know that they were in enemy territory. Any goods or livestock that they had managed to steal could not be got back across the dyke – not easily anyway. There are no known gateways the entire length of either Wat's or Offa's Dykes,' he said.

I asked him about the difference between the societies on either side of the dyke. David Hill said that they would have been fairly similar. The main difference was that the English side was all under the control of one ruler who had managed to take over the best land. The Welsh side was more tribal, with a large number of different groupings.

'But the people on the Welsh side would have been just as well, or badly, educated, just as skilful with their crafts and their agriculture. It was just a clash of culture and of language. Just as it is today in some areas,' said David Hill.

I had been with the archaeologists for over an hour and my mind kept on wandering back to Molly and whether she would be all right tied up. It was much the same feeling you get when you have left your car parked on a difficult bend or a yellow line. It is impossible to relax. You just feel that you ought to go and check on it. I thanked David Hill for his time. He did not seem to begrudge me it. As I walked back past the group of archaeologists they had decided to stop for lunch. The workers had become tea-drinkers and the shovel-leaners had disappeared – to the pub I suspect.

Molly was standing dozing where I had left her, but she was soon awake and ready to be heading back to Llanarmon. It was a beautiful valley with some good fertile land in the bottom around the river which snaked its way in towards the Welsh mountains. But the level, fertile bits were a fairly narrow strip. Most of the land was steeply banked up towards the hills. The farmers here would have been forced to be herders and shepherds – they still are. The large areas of good arable land are always on the English side of the dyke, leaving the Welsh with these attractive, but difficult to work, valleys. As I travelled down the borders, the best land was nearly always on my left and the worst on my right. Clearly the Welsh had always got the short end of the stick.

Wars between the English and the Welsh continued for another 500 years after Offa. The wars were always over territory. The dyke acted as a sealed border for a couple of hundred years, but later on there were periods when some interaction across the dyke was tolerated. One of the books I found in Ruthin Records Office dealt with the border and its operation. During the tenth century there were some very strict laws in force at the southern end of the border down near Abergavenny.

People were allowed to cross to the other side, but only if they were accompanied at all times by someone from the host nation. Just to ensure good conduct, you understand. The document reveals a deep distrust between the two nations on either side of the dyke:

Neither is a Welshman to cross over into English land, nor an Englishman to Welsh, without the appointed man from that land, who shall meet him at the bank and bring him back there again without any offence.

A Welshman conducting an Englishman around, or an Englishman conducting a Welshman around, would be held responsible for his guest's actions. If anything was stolen he would have to pay up on his guest's behalf. Most telling is the different value put on each other's heads. At that time if a crime was committed, say someone was killed, then a wergild had to be paid. This was a sum of money or goods which had to be given to the victim's family. The rate varied according to his status. The tenth-century border agreement covered the situation should there be a cross-border crime:

If a Welshman kills an Englishman he need not pay over this side more than half the man-price; no more than an Englishman for a Welshman to the other side, whether he be thane-born or churl-born; half the wergild falls away.

So, in plain English, here is the deal. If you cross the border you have to persuade a native to stay with you. Secondly, if you get involved in a scrap your life is only worth half what it would be if you had been bumped on the head when at home. These sort of rules may have allowed trade, but they did not actually encourage it.

But how much was a man worth? Later on, the document suggests that a stallion is worth 30 shillings, a mare 20 shillings, an ox 30 pence, a sow 24 pence. The man fits on this scale at 20 shillings, the same as the mare.

My mare was putting her 20-shillings' worth of effort into getting home at a fantastic lick. She had clearly decided that she wanted to get back to her friend and the new foal as quickly as possible. I must have been oblivious of the strong bond which had built up between the two horses over the previous few months. Breaking it would be a traumatic experience for all three of us.

On my way back through the village I stopped to phone my wife,

Jill. She had been unable to find a self-drive horsebox to hire in Wales. In the end she had found one at Bedford – about forty miles from home. I would have to go and pick it up the following evening. She had also found out about the trains from the borders to Bedford. It was not going to be an easy journey, needing four different trains.

I left Llanarmon early the next morning and very soon got a lift down to the bottom of the valley. The train trip took nearly the whole of the day and I arrived at Bedford tired and angry. The smells and the frustrations and the aggravations created by an excess of people brought me right back into the twentieth century.

Driving the van after so long in the saddle felt really odd. Everything was moving so fast. Other vehicles came careering out of side roads in front of me, oncoming cars whizzed inches away from my wing mirrors. By the time I got to Llanarmon it was gone 11.00 p.m. I was wound up like a coiled spring and wondering why the hell I had engaged on such a stupid project as to ride two stupid horses through the stupid borders when I could have been at home, in my own bed with my own wife. I was almost back to my normal, irrational, short-tempered, unpleasant self; but ten minutes after that I was sitting beside the tent in a remote field in Wales. There was no moon but the stars were dazzling, made brighter by the complete absence of artificial light. The trees were silhouettes of blackness against the sparkling sky. As I sipped tea, my eyes became accustomed to the darkness. I could make out the river by the stars reflected on its surface. I saw two shapes coming towards me through the darkness. The soft clamping of their feet on the turf was half heard with my ears and half felt through my body in contact with the ground. As the lumps came closer they resolved themselves into horses. At first I could not see the foal, but as they approached I could just make out her spindly shape walking between the massive bulks of Kate and Molly.

The aggravations of the day of twentieth-century travel fell into a sort of perspective. I got undressed and hunkered down into my sleeping bag. I remember hearing the foal suckling before I dropped off to sleep.

Chapter Ten

Tired legs, lost eyes, tame hares and Inspector Clouseau

I drove home to Buckinghamshire slightly slower than the average milk float, aware that if Kate lost her footing in the horsebox she could come crashing down on her foal. I felt sorry for the people who got stuck behind us, and received some dirty looks from drivers who eventually managed to get past. The trip took nearly five hours, and Kate was bursting with milk by the time I unloaded the two of them in the field behind my house. The foal was more than ready to relieve the pressure on her mother's udder.

I spent the night at home and then dropped the van off back at Bedford in time to catch the first of the four trains back to Oswestry station. By early afternoon I was back in the field and trying to come to terms with my forthcoming walk. I had lost nearly a week with the birth of the foal. The journey had come to a grinding halt and I had completed less than half of the distance to the Severn Bridge. That night I lay in the tent listening to Molly grazing close by and wondering how she would cope with just me for company.

I did not wake up until eight o'clock the next morning. There was no Kate pleading to be fed. I got up and called Molly over for her food. She did not have to come far as she had spent most of the night grazing close to the tent. By nine I had packed up and was ready to be off. By 9.30 I was through the village and had made a good start on the long slow climb up and across the flank of Mynydd Tarw. I had chosen a road route across to Penybontfawr, which is about thirteen miles south of Llanarmon. Thirteen miles seemed like a good distance for a first day's walk – well, it did before I started actually walking. The terrain was wide and rolling, the hills were grass covered with few trees. It would have been great to drive, to watch the scenery rolling by as the perspective changed on the humps and lumps in the distance. But I was on foot, and progress was slow. I fell into the dreaded walking trance. My mind drifted. I thought back to the day I had gone to Hereford horse auction to buy Molly. I had already bought Kate, and was running out of time for buying the second horse. An auction seemed like the best option. In horse circles, however, buying at auction is generally considered to be a pretty stupid thing to do – especially for someone who knows very little about horses.

In the past there was a simple rule governing horse sales: 'What you see is what you get.' There were no comebacks, there was no redress. Even the description in the catalogue did not have to be accurate. Now it does have to be more or less true – although it can be the sort of truth you get in a legal document or in an estate agent's description of a house. Estate agents could learn a lot from horse dealers. Phrases which seem to say a lot, but actually mean nothing at all, are frequently employed – 101% in traffic, an armchair ride, believed to have seen hounds, bombproof, sweet-natured, great character. Out of 200 horses at Hereford horse auction, Molly stood out as ideal.

All change from here on in – just me and Molly and another 130 miles to the Severn Bridge.

No 22   Molly, Chestnut Mare, 9 yrs, 15.2HH
A grand type of Irish-bred heavyweight Cob, mainly used as a hack
for elderly gentleman. Snaffle mouth and good comfortable paces.
Quiet to ride. Has been out with hounds, but not used to full
potential recently. Being sold as owner no longer able to ride.

Standing in the pen, with her clipped mane, stubby legs, big head and
barrel chest, Molly was no stunner. But she looked dead right.
Tough, quiet and ugly, nine-year-old Molly should have been getting
pretty wise about the ways of the world. She should have been
settling down nicely.

Two hours out from Llanarmon, I decided to stop for a break at
what I fondly hoped would be halfway. On consulting the map I
realised that I had done less than a third of the distance so far. My feet
felt fine but my legs were aching. I tied Molly up, unloaded her, and
flopped down on the ground for a rest. An hour whizzed past and I
forced myself to get up, load up and get under way again. I soon managed to walk the stiffness out of my legs. I got to a largish village called
Llanrhaeadr-ym-Mochnant which seems to have quite a lot of pubs. I
successfully passed the first one and congratulated myself on not
stopping. A few yards later I came across another pub, thought about
stopping, thought better of it and carried on. Then I came to the
third. My will cracked, I found a place to tie Molly and went in.
Thirty minutes and two pints later I was back under way, with the
alcohol anaesthetising the complaints from my legs. I floated the rest
of the way to Penybontfawr.

Penybontfawr has two caravan parks and several pubs. The
countryside is nice enough but nothing special. Once I had sorted
Molly out and pitched the tent I nipped down to the village shop to
buy some food. There was a sign on the door advertising a concert in
St Thomas's church in aid of the roof repair fund – I wonder if
churches raise money for anything else. A male voice choir was coming from Trawsfynydd, a village on the other side of the Berwyn
mountains.

I bought a ticket and two hours later joined the crowd of villagers, plus a few tourists, squeezing themselves onto the hard oak pews in the church. The concert was due to start at 7.30, but at 7.45 the choir had still not shown up. At ten to eight a group of thirty men, dressed in matching fawn-coloured jackets, came in and sat in the choir stalls. They covered the complete spectrum of ages from spotty youths to old men.

A formidable, black-garbed lady preacher stood at the pulpit and addressed the audience in Welsh – at some considerable length. Eventually she launched into an abbreviated English version of what I assumed was more or less the same speech.

Then the leader of the male voice choir stood up. He also gave an interminable speech in Welsh which apparently contained three screamingly funny jokes. It had the villagers of Penybontfawr rolling in the aisles. The non-Welsh speakers in the audience could only smile politely. I looked forward to hearing the jokes in English but they must have lost something in the translation. One appeared to be a remark about the heather on the mountains being in flower the last time the choir came here. Another was about the way that the choir was under strength at this time of year because the farmer members were too busy making hay.

I thought that the concert was due to start when the Welsh soliloquy started again. There were more rib-ticklingly funny jokes for the Welsh speakers. I was hoping that this time they would be as good in English. They were not. Perhaps there is something inherently funny about there being a garage proprietor, a fish farmer and a headmaster in the same choir but only if it is told in Welsh. Just the faintest hint of linguistic paranoia started to creep into my mind. Were they having a good laugh at the expense of the non-Welsh speakers in the audience? I could see why English people who came here felt the need to learn Welsh. The reason was not to placate the Welsh but to ensure their own mental stability.

It reminded me of the time I saw one of the Pink Panther films in a cinema in Paris. The English people in the audience were in hysterics at Peter Sellers's crummy French accent. The French people in the audience, with only the subtitles to help them, were convinced that they were the victims of a conspiracy.

Around eight o'clock the singing finally got under way. It was wonderful. I used to sing in the choir at school. There is a tremendous feeling of power when standing in the middle of a group of men giving of their vocal best. The bass notes from your own vocal cords, added to those from the people around you, reverberate around your chest. Before the choir had started singing they had looked almost bored at the prospect of giving yet another concert, but once they started they remembered why they were doing it. Their sense of exuberance came through. The smiles on their faces grew broader as they could see the effect they were having on the audience. The repertoire was extensive and included psalms and hymns as well as country-and-western songs in Welsh.

All through my trip I had come across music, song and poetry. The English seem quite content to appreciate music rather than make it. The Welsh feel a need to join in – and with such consummate skill.

I was settling back to my passive appreciation when it was announced that we would all stand and join in a well-known hymn. The organisers had been kind enough to print the words on the back of the programme so that none of us could be excused from joining in. The first two lines were as follows:

> Bro'r goleuni, Salem nefol,
> Dinas pur dangnefedd Duw,

The next thirty-four lines were no easier. I stood there mouthing like a self-conscious goldfish while the audience around me gave the choir as good as they had been getting all evening. I noticed that the choir used this opportunity to pick out the non-Welsh speakers in the audience and have a little chuckle at their expense.

After the concert I walked back to the field where I had pitched the tent and left Molly. She trotted over to greet me as I came back through the gate – something she would never have bothered to do when she had Kate for company. The weather forecast for the next day was good, the field where Molly and I were staying had excellent grass and I thought that we could justify a day off. Actually I thought my legs could do with a day off. Molly did not need a day off at all. She was getting really fit and was muscling up like a warhorse. My fears about her losing weight on the trip were completely unfounded. Physically she was thriving, although I was worried about how she would adjust to life with just me for company.

Although I had found the previous day's walk exhausting, it had been a bit of a holiday for Molly. She was carrying the pack which was much lighter than I was. In addition she had to walk at my pace which was much slower than her own natural pace. She seemed full of energy and was raring to go so I thought that a ride of a few miles would be good for both of us.

While I was in the shop at Penybontfawr the previous night I had picked up a little booklet about a local saint called Melangell. She had lived in a little hermitage four or five miles away, just the other side of Llangynog. Her shrine seemed an obvious choice for an outing.

After half an hour or so Molly settled down to a steady pace and the two of us watched the scenery roll by. I started to think about St Melangell in particular and Welsh saints in general. There does seem to be a huge number of them. One book I found listed ninety-three. They span the alphabet from St Aelhaearn of Caernarvonshire to St Ystyffan of Radnorshire. The list did not even mention St Melangell. Welsh saints appear to have a monopoly on bizarre life stories. One, St Illtyd, managed to invent the plough 600 years after the Romans brought it to Britain. He also had an animal which was half horse, half stag, which he took on shopping expeditions. A favourite of mine, St Ffraid, has a life story which is an uncomfortable blend of Mills and Boon and *Nightmare on Elm Street*. Ffraid was an Irish virgin whose father wanted her to marry an Irish lord. She didn't like the look of the Irish lord very much, so she made herself unmarriageable by pulling her own eyes out. However, she was not as daft as you might think because she kept them in her pocket, and when no one was looking (how did she know no one was looking?), she washed them and stuck them back in. This bizarre behaviour was not enough to put the Irish lord off so Ffraid cut a sod of Irish earth and rowed it to Wales.

Apart from inventing the sport of sod-yachting, St Ffraid also managed to carve herself a career as a miracle worker. She created miracles the way most people make cups of tea. Her stepmother lost a leg on a visit to a nunnery so St Ffraid grew her another one.

I wanted to talk to the vicar who was in charge of the church dedicated to one of these strange Welsh saints and ask him how he squared the behaviour of his patron saint with the theology of modern Christianity.

The last bit of the journey was up a single-track road which went nowhere other than the small cluster of houses by the church. The valley has a perfectly level bottom which is now down to improved pastures. The flood-plain soil, which had been stripped off the hills above us and spread across the valley bottom, is obviously very fertile; the grass is lush and green. There are lots of strong mature trees scattered around the valley. Everything was so perfect it was almost as

Travelling with a packhorse can be perfect.

though it had been designed that way – a landscape gardener's idea of a rural idyll. Of course, good weather and a general feeling of well-being were helping things along greatly. Perhaps walking the rest of the journey would not be so bad after all.

The chapel dedicated to St Melangell is nothing special at all. Just an old Welsh House of God. There are ones like it everywhere. It is the surroundings which make it unique. It is a place designed for sitting and thinking. A couple of men were working on the building when I arrived, repointing the brickwork. The gentle scrape of their trowels as they raked out and replaced the mortar between the brick joints added to the feeling of peace and quiet. Mercifully, they had forgone the pleasures of a ghetto blaster, Radio One and *Steve Wright in the Afternoon.*

I tied Molly up and went off to find the vicar who, the church board told me, was called Paul Davies. I found him in his garden, deadheading the daffodils. He was an old man, slightly stooped, with grey hair and grey bushy Denis Healey eyebrows. He had a very English voice, quiet and soft. He said that he was quite happy to show me the chapel and to tell me about it. He shuffled off to get the key which turned out to be a real monster, eight inches long and decorated with bands and hoops along its length. Even the business end was more a wrought-iron pattern than a shape to fool a lock picker. The key had that dull lustre objects take on when they have been used for decades. I felt the desire to hold it in my hand, to feel the time-dulled edges for myself. Merely to look at such an object is only to appreciate the half of it. There is a great pleasure to be had by placing your hand, your fingers, where previous generations have placed theirs. As we walked slowly over towards the chapel I asked the Reverend Davies if I could hold the key. He seemed to understand why I should ask.

It was only a fifty-yard walk from house to chapel but Mr Davies had to stop at the lich gate to get his breath back. He was obviously suffering from severe respiratory problems. That may have accounted for his quiet, gentle voice, but I suspected that he had always spoken that way. I am sure that people would have listened very carefully to his sermons as much for the pleasure of the voice as the quality of the message.

When he got to the chapel, he opened the door to show me the inside of the church – the pews were out, and the floor was up. He pointed out a few of the main features and then we went outside to talk. He carefully lowered himself onto a grave which was in a sun trap created by the wall of the church and the side of the porch and invited me to sit beside him on the dark slab of granite. It had been soaking up the heat of the sun all morning and was pleasantly warm to the touch. I could just see Molly from where we were sitting. The men had gone to lunch and even their quiet work noises were no longer there to disturb the peace. I could not think of a better place to be than right there.

'I suppose you want to know about Melangell,' he said, pronouncing the 'll' at the end by putting his tongue against the roof of his mouth and blowing air at his molars. When I nodded, he took a deep breath and started on the tale of the Irish noblewoman called Monacella, who eventually became St Melangell. She had been betrothed to a young man of a good family, but Monacella did not want the marriage, so she resolved to run away to a place where she could not be found. She is supposed to have rowed to Wales in a coracle. She eventually found this valley where she settled down as a hermit, living off the land and caring for the wild animals. She is supposed to have struck up a particular rapport with hares.

One day Brochwel, Prince of Powys, came up to the valley on a hunting expedition. His hounds raised a hare and set off in pursuit. It took refuge under Monacella's skirts. She ordered the dogs not to pursue it any more. Prince Brochwel was impressed with this young woman, her pure lifestyle and the sanctuary she had created for these animals. He decreed that the valley should be a sanctuary for anyone who needed refuge and helped Monacella to establish a nunnery.

Paul told the story without much embellishment and with a wry smile on his face.

'And how much of that is true?' I asked.

'Not much,' he said, as the laugh which had been waiting to get out finally emerged. 'We do know that a church was established here by a woman in the fifth or sixth century. The Irish were evangelising in this part of Wales at this time, so there is a good chance that she could have been Irish. People living in quiet spots like this often get on well with the local wildlife and Welsh princes would have spent a lot of their time hunting. So who knows?'

I asked him about the Welsh saints and why there were so many of them.

Paul told me that unofficial saints are not unique to Wales. They can be found all over the world. Very few are recognised in Rome. I asked him why the Irish connection was so common.

'You see, Irish priests were active in the east of the country trying to convert the Welsh to Christianity, while other Irishmen were making raids on the coast. The Irish Sea has never been much of a barrier to either Christian or un-Christian endeavour.'

More recent missionaries to Africa have adapted Christianity to fit in with local customs so perhaps the same sort of thing was going on in Wales. There is little doubt that this place was a holy site hundreds of years before Monacella or Melangell came here. It was common practice to build Christian churches on top of the old holy sites. Animal worship was common. If Monacella could demonstrate power over animals, then that might have helped her a great deal. Even a few local chieftains might have found it useful to claim supernatural powers derived from God. The legend and the stories take over, and the whole lot becomes mixed up in a confusion of myth and reality.

So what of the nunnery, did that ever exist?

'It seems doubtful. There are no records of it. If it did, it probably did not last for long after her death. But Cwm Pennant did become a place of pilgrimage. Eventually the Normans built a stone church on the site,' said Paul. As he was speaking his fingers were tracing the letters on the slab we were using as a seat. I asked if the Richard Davies whose grave we were borrowing was any relation. Paul assured me that he was not, but he hoped that Richard would not mind us sharing this sunny spot with him for a while.

But why would the Normans have bothered building churches this far into hostile territory?

'They used the Church as an instrument of invasion. They took over the Church before taking over politically. Their conquering was done as much with the cross as with the sword. They did not really bother taking over this area, but they did need to know what was going on in case trouble and discontent were brewing. The Church would have acted as an intelligence-gathering agency. The strong church buildings fulfilled another function for them. The Normans might have needed to make raids deep into enemy territory. A few easily-defended stone buildings such as this could have been very useful for a military operation.'

We sat in silence for a moment or two while I thought about the place behind me being used for military purposes. Paul was one of those people with whom a silence is not an intrusion. He seemed quite content to let me think about and absorb what he had said. I looked at the ranks of gravestones in the yard around us. I wondered out loud if the crowded graveyard was an indication of a crowded church on Sundays.

A wheezy laugh escaped from Paul's chest. 'No, I have a much larger congregation of gravestones than people. But who nowadays does not? Of course, in the old days, before 1600, graveyards were never crowded. People were just buried in unmarked graves in the consecrated ground.'

I suggested that churchyards must have been much nicer places for it.

'Yes, yes, I suppose they were. But then we would not have anything to sit on, would we?'

Chapter Eleven

Lost again, sent away, and the gentle art of the flower judge

I could see from the map that there was a bridle path heading due south from Penybontfawr. I had learned to become wary of untried or unrecommended bridle paths, but the only alternative route would take us four miles along the main road, so I decided that it was worth the risk. After all, I only had one horse to deal with now and overhanging branches could no longer force me to get off and walk as I was already on foot. I should have known better – especially as the path ran through forestry land.

It started off very nicely by following a steep road leading to a farm. I asked at the farm about the bridleway and whether it was possible to get through. The farmer told me that a lady had gone up it on a horse just a couple of weeks ago. I suppose I should have asked him if she ever came back. However, I pushed on along the edge of a field and then followed a sign into the forestry land. Within a few hundred yards the trees started to close in so tightly on either side that the lower branches were snagging on Molly's pack. The track got worse and worse with wind-blown trees blocking the route, forcing me to work out diversions even deeper into the trees. We battled on, trying to find a way through. The track, such as it was, eventually crossed a forestry dirt road. I could see the bridleway I was following going on through the trees. It looked in even worse shape than the bit I had used already. I decided to give up on it and follow the forestry road instead. It took me in almost every direction but the one I wanted to travel. Three hours later I managed to get back to the safety of the road. I had progressed a mere two miles.

Molly and I carried on along the road. It was really rather nice, with trees lining both sides. There was the occasional glimpse of fields between them and, every now and again, a secluded house. Good places to live where the neighbours were a decent dog's walk away from you. The sun came out and the birds started singing. Actually, I suspect that they had been singing all along. It was just that my head had been so full of evil thoughts about foresters that there was no room left to appreciate the birds. In my calmer state I remembered that I was doing the journey for the sake of travel, not for the sake of getting somewhere. I decided that I would try to regard the next locked gate or blocked path as an opportunity for another pleasant diversion. It would allow me to see countryside and views I would otherwise have missed. Great things, resolutions.

A pack's-eye view of a hack in the borders.

It was now 11.30 and I had about fifteen miles still to do. I had decided to head for a place called Castle Caereinion, not because it was anything special, but it did have four things in its favour. First, it had a pub. Second, it was only four miles from Welshpool, where the Montgomeryshire County Show was being held the next day. Third, it was seven miles from Montgomery where I wanted to spend an afternoon. Fourth, and quite important this one, it was the last village on the last map I had with me. I had thought that a walk of fifteen or sixteen miles should have been well within my capacity, but I had not reckoned with the six or seven extra miles getting lost in the forest. We did not get to Castle Caereinion until after six in the evening.

I called in at several farms to see if I could put up for the night and was told with varying degrees of politeness to go away. Somehow, now that I was on foot, people had started to treat me differently. It had taken three attempts to get somewhere to stay at Penybontfawr; now I was having no luck at all. Walkers clearly command less respect and trust than people on horseback. On my way down from Penybontfawr I had noticed a few travelling people in vans and old cars – perhaps I was being categorised as just another drop-out. With some sadness I walked past Castle Caereinion, on down the road towards Montgomery and off the edge of the map . . . Now I only had my eyes to tell me what was coming up. It was odd not knowing what lay ahead. All I knew was that Montgomery was seven miles away because that had been marked on the bottom margin.

A mile on down the road I came to a farm which had one or two promising fields around it. The yard was empty and I walked around shouting, to see if anyone was around. The house seemed empty, too. I was so tired that I was tempted to squat in one of the fields for the night, but I knew that I would not sleep well for fear that someone would come and rant at me for trespassing – and they would be entirely right to do so.

I was just about to turn away and carry on towards Montgomery when a mob of sheep came down the road. A young boy was walking in front of them shaking a bag of feed under the noses of the leaders, while a man in a pick-up followed behind, shouting and whistling at a couple of working sheepdogs. The procession turned into the yard and the man got out of his truck smiling. It was nice to see a smile. Richard said that I was welcome to pitch my tent in one of his fields.

I ate a meal of mush. This one said vegetable risotto on the pack. I don't know why I bothered reading or even looking at the label. The instructions, the cooking time and the end result were exactly the same each time. My instant meals were the gastronomic equivalent of a Mills and Boon book – mushy, unsatisfying and always with the same ending. Only the packaging was different.

I slept well that night, except for waking up a couple of times to hear Molly grazing by the tent. I reckoned that I could estimate the length of grass by the sound of her grazing. It was a relaxing noise. I dropped off to sleep, wondering whether her legs were aching as much as mine.

I woke early and headed off towards Welshpool and the Montgomeryshire Show. I left Molly in the field grazing beside the tent.

The show was being held in a massive pasture beside the main Ludlow road. The field had a long gentle slope which levelled out at the bottom into a flat area about the size of two or three rugby pitches. Land in Wales should be measured in rugby pitch equivalents – not football pitches. The slope offers a natural grandstand. No one has an excuse for not seeing what is going on in the main ring.

County shows are wonderful institutions run by dedicated groups of masochists. It is the only explanation for why they do it. Their first problem is the weather. Some shows seem to be blessed with good weather every year, and others have the rain follow them around whatever the date. For some shows it can be fine right up to the day of the show when, bang on time, the heavens will open. The Montgomeryshire Show used to be held in September. They suffered an unbroken run of rain-struck events, so the show was moved to the beginning of June – not a step to be taken lightly. Many county show cups are closely linked to certain seasons; it is hard to produce prize-winning onions or tomatoes in June.

I paid my entrance fee and walked through the light drizzle onto the showground. As usual, the weatherman was not being kind to the Montgomeryshire Show and its committee. It was 10.30 in the morning and there did not seem to be that many members of the public at the show. The exhibitors and competitors had been there for hours – preening, polishing, arranging, brushing and plaiting. A group of people were standing in the doorway of a small marquee looking philosophically disconsolate as they watched drips falling off the roof and into the wet ground. The word 'Committee' was written in white letters on a blue board nailed to a stake just in front of their tent.

A First World War German show organ mounted on the back of a Bedford TK lorry was being made to play patriotic British war songs. The punch cards were being fed into its interior by its proud owner – an unnaturally thin, elderly man. He told me that he was there every year. He offered to do requests.

' "Congratulations", "Quando Quando", "A Walk in the Black Forest", I've got all the modern ones,' he said when I spoke to him.

Mr Bishop became insistent. 'Ask me, go on, ask me. I've got the lot.'

I asked for 'Amazing Grace' because the choir at Penybontfawr had sung it so nicely two nights before. I was confident that 'Amazing Grace' was not the sort of song a fairground organ could be made to play. Mr Bishop smiled hugely, disappeared into the bowels of his organ, and re-emerged with a new set of punch cards. Unbelievably, his smile had grown larger. The tune was hardly recognisable once it had the Germanic oompah cymbal-clashing tones of the organ imposed on it. The cymbal-waving monkeys, clowns and spinning mechanical ballet dancers moved manically through their routines just as they had for 'Pack Up Your Troubles' and 'It's A Long Way To Tipperary'. It made Mr Bishop happy. John Newton, the man who wrote 'Amazing Grace', must have been pinwheeling in his grave.

Mr Bishop dragged me round the back of his lorry and up a short flight of steps to show me his punch-card library. He hustled me into a very narrow corridor. It must have been less than eighteen inches wide and ran the full length of the lorry. The noise from the organ was unbelievable – not only the tune, but also the grinding, whirring, clicking and ratcheting of its working parts. The other side of the corridor was made up of shelves, stacked from floor to ceiling with Mr Bishop's precious punch cards. The passage was so narrow I had to turn sideways to squeeze in. Mr Bishop came in behind me. I felt like a trapped animal as he kept on talking to me all the time, pushing me further into the bowels of his demented machine, showing me cards and titles as we went. Occasionally he would rush towards the exit end to get some cards and come skating back to show them to me. He was shouting titles out all the time, even when his back was turned. The organ was so loud I could not hear a word he was saying. After a couple of minutes of this, the organ suddenly fell silent. Mr Bishop ran down his corridor and disappeared down the steps. I shuffled sideways towards the beckoning daylight and open air.

As I walked down the steps to freedom Mr Bishop caught me again. He told me that he did not know what would happen to the organ once he was too old to care for it. He hoped that he could find someone who would look after it the way he had, but it needed to be the right sort of person. A thin one, for starters.

I made my excuses and left. I bought a coffee and drank it while studying the catalogue. There were 126 classes for farm livestock alone. They ranged from in-milk heifers to a class for two-ewe lambs. There were also sixty-three different classes for horses ranging from the tiny in-hand ponies to decorated heavy horses.

I decided to hide away from the drizzle and sought refuge in the flower tent where the judging was already under way. The flower judge, a very dapper man called Kevin Gunnel, was just finishing his morning's work. He had been brought in from Shropshire for the job. Flower people find it 'more convenient', he said, to import judges from other associations.

'It avoids upset, you see,' said Mr Gunnel in his quiet, precise

*The show cob is the last bastion of men in
the female-dominated world of horses.*

voice. His job was a hard one, having to pick positions one, two and
three from half a dozen entries in the flower-arranging classes. One of
the subjects today was 'The Conservatory'. The design had to
symbolise and convey some essence of a conservatory, he told me.
Hardest of all, he had to make comments on each arrangement –
'striking the right note between honesty and encouragement', as he
put it.

I asked him what he was looking for in a good arrangement and he
launched into an excited monologue on the finer points of flower
arranging. He pointed to lines of symmetry my eye failed to detect,
and disastrous dissymmetry to which I was equally blind. One entry
was marked down because a few grains of yellow pollen had been
knocked out of the stamens and onto the white petals. Surely an act
of nature, but one Mr Gunnel believed should have been avoided by
wrapping each stamen in tissue paper before subjecting the arrangement to the car journey. Other, more successful, competitors had
taken the time and trouble to do so. Mr Gunnel said that he could do

no other than to reward the stamen wrappers for their diligence. Another arrangement was condemned for its 'floral clash of personalities'.

It seemed that you had to be a hard, unforgiving sort of person to be a judge of flower arrangements. Mr Gunnel was gently unforgiving in his judgements.

'I have been on the receiving end of some abuse,' he admitted with a smile. It was at Windsor, in the Royal County of Berkshire no less, that an irate husband had grabbed Mr Gunnel by the lapel and asked him to explain the hard comments he had made about a particular arrangement. The unfortunate husband's life had been a living hell for the previous few days as his wife whipped herself into a competitive frenzy, spending a modest-sized fortune and every spare minute on getting ready for the event. The husband had been driven from his bed at 3.30 a.m. to get his wife and her precious cargo to the showground by 4.30 in the morning. The husband had dined on bread and cheese the night before the event and had been offered no breakfast at all. The sole reward for all this effort was a few lines of Mr Gunnel's pithy prose on the back of a yellow card. Mr Gunnel's comments had driven the Wife of Windsor to tears. The husband was not far behind.

'But I cannot let such considerations stand in my way,' said Mr Gunnel. 'No, I must not,' he said, as much to himself as to me.

By now it had stopped raining, so I went back up to the livestock lines where the cattle judging was under way. A line of similar-looking black and white cattle stood patiently beside their white-coated owners. A judge ran his hand and his eye over each one in turn. The cattle that is. At least with the flowers I could see the differences between the arrangements. The cows looked like peas from a pod, apart from their markings. The right-hand side of one cow looked amazingly like a map of North America with the land in black and the ocean in white. I spent a few minutes looking for more geographical freaks.

I fell into conversation with a man propping his bottom off the ground on a shooting stick. He tried to explain what the judge was looking for; but he soon realised that he was talking to an idiot. I did learn from him that most of the owners would have been rubbing chalk into the white bits and blackening-up the black bits to increase the contrast. It was perfectly legal, but they were running a risk should it come on to rain again.

That took our conversation on to cheating. He said that a bit of blacking-up was nothing. Apparently, the biggest shake-up for the dairy cow show-ring had come in the 1950s with the introduction of the machine milker. In the old days, when cows were milked by hand, the ideal udder shape was a big bag with large, generous, hand-sized teats like German sausages sticking out on each side of the udder. Nice and easy to get at – eminently squeezable. A pint in three pulls was the ideal. Then along came the milking machine. That required a complete change in udder shape with much smaller teats sticking straight down, one on each corner like stubby table legs. Almost overnight, whole cattle-breeding dynasties collapsed. Men whose cattle were valued in thousands of pounds suddenly found that no one wanted their animals any more.

Desperate measures were taken and a new show-ring preparation procedure was developed. The cow would be milked out at about three in the morning and a rubber solution called 'Collodion' painted over the udder. Then an udder-sized cardboard box, with four holes cut in the bottom for the teats, would be strapped to the cow. As she filled up with milk the udder would take on this perfect square box shape. A few minutes before entering the ring, the box would be removed and the rubber solution would hold the udder in shape long enough to get through the showing procedure.

I did not believe the man when he told me all this, but I have checked it since. It is all true and, what is even more extraordinary, at the time it was perfectly legal.

Chapter Twelve

Swearing farmers, dispassionate facts of killing and immoral railway bosses

Molly seemed quite happy in Richard's field. There were a few sheep around, and they seemed to act as company for her – although you must be pretty desperate for company if you are down to regarding sheep as friends. Molly had also changed her attitude towards me and was becoming much more interested in my comings and goings. She would graze close to the tent at night and follow me across the field when I went over to get water. When I came back from the Montgomeryshire Show she whinnied a welcome at me. It would have been quite flattering, but I knew that this attention was motivated by loneliness.

We made a late start, but it was only a short six-mile walk to Montgomery and Molly was trying to overtake me all the way there. Most of the trip was along a B road, although it was so quiet it was really little more than a lane. It took us through a village called Berriew. Their Montgomeryshire Show 'It's a Knockout' team had been accused of cheating in the six young farmers in a woolsack competition.

Berriew is a nice little place, with a decent-sized church, old narrow streets and a river with a satisfyingly ancient stone bridge over it. The centre of the village was busy in a quietly rural sort of way. Decent respectable beige-dressed women carrying decent respectable proper shopping bags were in evidence. People greeted each other and greeted me – no questions, no staring, just a well-spoken

'Good morning'. I felt that I was surrounded by the sort of genteel politeness a person could drown in. One shop had a sign saying 'Family Butcher' written on a blue board over the top. A slightly sinister name for a shop, that.

Molly and I crossed the Berriew stone bridge, the note of her clip clop rising and falling as we walked over the arches. I stopped to talk to a man who was contemplating the river. We talked about the water, the weather and the world for about ten minutes. He never once mentioned Molly, or her pack, or asked me where I was going. Berriew did not seem to be a place for gossiping and inquiring about other people's business – not in public anyway.

After the bridge we turned left along a road running alongside the river. Someone had written 'DEATH TO ALL FARMERS' in white paint on the road. The letters were big and square and precise.

A mile after Berriew we came to a T-junction onto the main trunk road between Welshpool and Newtown. We only had to do a mile of it. It was nearly our last mile together. A man in a red Ford Fiesta trying to overtake a lorry came screaming towards us on our side of the road. Molly, I, he and the lorry driver all thought something nasty was going to happen. Collisions between horses and cars are messy and usually fatal. The centre of gravity of a horse is about three feet from the ground – about the level of a car windscreen. The horse's legs break on impact and half a tonne of body comes in through the windscreen. At sixty miles an hour the man in the red Fiesta would not have had much chance. We all had a lucky escape.

As soon as we turned off the trunk road I stopped and tied Molly to a fence to contemplate my future – in particular its duration. I looked again at the map and noticed that I could have completely avoided the trunk road by travelling an extra mile along some back lanes. Next time I would take more care.

An hour later I was close enough to Montgomery to start looking for a place to stay. I called in at one farm and walked around self-consciously shouting 'Hello', but the only answer I got was from some cows in a yard.

I walked on, past a sewage farm, which upset both Molly and me. I could hear a forage harvester working over in the distance and walked towards the noise. The driver was just finishing hoovering up the last of the grass in the field. He said that we were welcome to make use of it for a day or two. There was plenty of grass left around the edge of the field where the machinery could not reach.

I had been told back in Penybontfawr that if you want to learn anything about the town of Montgomery then there is just one man to see. His name is Ivor Tanner. Unfortunately, my instructions for finding him were pathetic.

'Go into the main square at Montgomery. There is a pub there. I forget what it is called. Ask anyone in there to tell you where you can find Ivor Tanner.' I have played this sort of game before and always come unstuck, but it was all I had to go on. I found the pub, and asked at the bar for Ivor Tanner. The barman certainly knew of him and said that it would be worth trying at Ivor's house. I found the house easily enough. Ivor had moved. Try the castle. Where is the castle? On top of the hill. They usually are. It was a very steep hill. A very, very steep hill.

Twenty minutes later, sweating, panting and with aching calves, I arrived at Montgomery Castle. I was convinced that I was wasting my time. A group of men were drinking tea in a small green shed. Three of them were called Tanner and one of them was called Ivor. And from him I learnt almost nothing about Montgomery, but I did gain an insight into the art of building castles.

Ivor said that he could spare me ten minutes to tell me about Montgomery so we left his colleagues and cousins in the green hut with their Thermos flasks, plastic lunch boxes and Old Holborn. We leant against one of the crumbling parapets of the castle. Ivor is a stonemason who works for CADW – the organisation which looks after all the castles on the Welsh side of the border. He was dressed in a tatty blue boiler suit. His slicked-back black hair and well-trimmed moustache gave him the look of a 1930s lounge lizard.

It must require a lot of skill to rebuild a castle, I said, by way of an opener and ice-breaker. Ivor fished a tobacco tin out of its usual resting place in his top pocket. The material kept its square shape, waiting for the tin's return. He opened it up and started rolling a cigarette – a very thin cigarette.

'Well,' he said, pausing to lick the sticky strip on the paper, 'well, laying bricks is a skill. Two good men will finish up with exactly the same end result. Two men can start at opposite ends of a wall and work towards each other and you'll never see the join. Stonemasonry is an entirely different thing. Stones and masons are individuals – each one different from the next, you see. There's no perfect, definitive place for each stone to go – only better and worse positions. There are no absolutes. It's an art.'

He told me that when he is rebuilding something he has to try and match the style and quality of the man who did the original work. Sometimes that may mean deliberately doing a bit less than your best.

'Show me,' I said, forgetting that the discussion about masonry was supposed to be no more than a diversion to get him talking.

Ivor lit his cigarette and took me across towards the centre of the castle where he pointed to a seventeenth-century dovecot, which he said had been built using stone taken from the thirteenth-century perimeter wall. Apparently a pretty lousy workman had been taken on to do the job. A cowboy was the word Ivor used, even though the

Ivor Tanner in 'his' castle at Montgomery.

work was done 200 years before the Americans would get around to inventing cowboys. The dovecot repairs were being done in the same style and with the same weak mix of limestone mortar. This repair would last only 150, perhaps 200 years. Ivor's repairs are normally expected to last 1000 or even 2000 years.

When Ivor is re-laying stones he is trying to get into the head of the man who did the original work. Only then can he place the stones in just the right position. If he fails to get it just right, even my uneducated eye will be able to see a subtle change in the pattern between the old and the new. When he is doing such work Ivor is in touch with the past in a way which few of us can ever hope to experience. He told me how on one occasion he put his hand up behind a cornice and found a carving on the back of a stone where no one could ever see it. Put there like a time capsule – a message across the centuries from one craftsman to another. Ivor finds himself doing the same thing from time to time.

During our ten minutes I learned about the 'sap' in a piece of sandstone – how the rock is soft and malleable when it has been cut fresh from the quarry, but once it has been removed from the mass of rock and given a decade or two to settle, it dries and hardens to a tool-blunting intractability. Ivor also showed me the stone dresser's marks which will have been carved into every stone that went into Montgomery Castle. He knows these marks, and he knows the men who made them, not by their names or their looks – he knows them better than that, he knows them by the quality of their work. He knows which masons have produced good results through long, slow chipping away at the stone. He knows other, bolder, more skilled men, who could produce well-dressed stones with a few bold strokes. Some masons' marks can always be found on blocks used at the most crucial positions where precision-made shapes for gateways, windows and arches are required. Others produced work fit only for the bulk of the curtain walls. Ivor can also trace the development of particular masons from apprentices to master masons. Some might have spent their whole lives working on the Castle.

Then there were the hauliers, who made their living bringing the rock from quarries ten miles away and the mortar from the lime pits fifteen miles away. They were the long-distance drivers of the past, doing a regular run with their ox-drawn carts. Out one day, stay overnight, and back the next. Men might have spent their lives travelling the same fifteen miles back and forth, watching the changes in the seasons and the seasons add up into years and the years mount up into decades – all from the seat of a creaking bullock cart. Not a bad job for a man with a lot of thinking to do. Not an unpleasant way to spend a life. Possibly a good deal better than working on a production line at Ford's.

I suggested that the architecture of castles seemed rather crude, just a compound surrounded by big fat walls – the bigger and fatter the better. Ivor's cigarette tin came out again, his fingers operating independently while he thought about how best to educate me.

Ivor explained that castles are built in a series of concentric defensive rings, and then pointed to the ditch behind the outer curtain wall. He described how they were designed to double up as storage areas and places to keep livestock in peacetime. When the castle was under attack they would be defended but, if necessary, yielded up to the enemy. But breaching these outer walls would have been a Pyrrhic victory for the attackers. They would find themselves in possession of death-trap trenches, vulnerable to three-way crossfire from the inner walls and towers above. Even the staircases were designed to offer maximum advantage to the defenders. They spiral down anticlockwise, giving a free swing for the sword arms of those above. The central pillar blocks the swing for the attackers coming up the stairs. The stairs must have been a horribly claustrophobic place in which to fight for your life. The castles are not only designed to protect those inside but to maximise the damage done to the attackers.

'The people inside could inflict terrible injuries on the attackers. A kill ratio of twenty to one or better was the aim,' said Ivor Tanner as he finished the last of his cigarette. Little wonder that sieges were preferable to assaults.

Montgomery Castle had come under siege several times. Prince Dafydd came close to taking it in 1234. In 1401 Owain Glyndwr, the hero of the twentieth-century Welsh nationalists, came here. He sacked the town, but left the castle because it was too big a nut to crack. Looking down into the town beneath us, every detail was clear – cars neatly parked in the market square, dogs tied up outside the supermarket, kids on bikes. The town was near enough to recognise individuals. You could even carry on a shouted conversation with them if your lungs were powerful enough. It must have been horrible to stand here watching houses being pillaged and burned by Glyndwr and his men.

'Not as horrible as being down there while it was being done,' said Ivor.

The next morning I woke to the sound of cars shushing along the road beside the field. It had been raining through most of the night and it was still raining when I turned on *Farming Today*. George was telling the listeners why the government had decided to put a health warning on unpasteurised milk. Then David Membury at the London Weather Centre told me that there was a 'generally unsettled look to the weather today, with some rain through most districts and some heavier spells of rain in the west'. By seven o'clock we were having one of those heavier spells. At 10.30 the weatherman's rainy spell was still going strong. It began to feel as though my tent was shrinking in the rain. I had yesterday's newspaper to read and was well into the obituaries. I was reassured to discover that just over forty-five per cent of the deceased had died peacefully in their sleep. Fifteen per cent of them had double-barrelled names. By 12.00 I had given up waiting for the rain to stop. I packed up the soggy tent and we were under way.

Five minutes later the sun came out.

I had planned a fifteen-mile walk to Bishop's Castle. The first part was to take me through an area of parkland just to the east of Montgomery, through to Church Stoke and then up along the Kerry Ridgeway, which should eventually take me down to Bishop's Castle.

It was wonderful to be released from the confinement of the tent. There is a tremendous freshness in the air when the rain stops. My route took me along a lane which snaked through the parkland, around a lake and past the most beautiful cricket pitch I have ever seen. There were tall, mature trees all around a lovely pavilion. Even I might be persuaded to support my local cricket team if they had a pitch such as this on which to play. My plan was to take the path along a section of Offa's Dyke which was marked as a bridleway, nip down a short length of farm road and then onto a back lane to Church Stoke.

The last bit of the road through the parkland dipped under some trees where the birds were singing as though there was no tomorrow. I presumed that they too had spent a frustrating morning waiting for the rain to finish. I stopped to listen and to marvel at the sound and at the sight of the sun filtering down through the green June leaves. The rhythm of the journey was getting to me. In my real existence I would never have spared ten minutes just to listen to birds and look at sunbeams. Ten minutes was a lot of time to spend doing anything which did not earn money. After such a lousy start to the day things were turning out so well. I wished that more of the trip could have been through scenery like this. I should have known.

Just where I expected it to be (oh, what a perfect day it was turning out to be!), there was a gate off to the right. At first all I could see was a hedgeline on top of a slight rise. When I got closer I realised that this was the dyke itself, marked merely by a slight depression on my side, the Welsh side, and the hedge-topped bank on the English side. As I approached the gateway, I noticed that it was padlocked. Curses! My way ahead was also blocked because a cattle-grid had been installed across the road, preventing me from going onwards. I was hugely upset. I was swearingly, cursingly, angrily upset. I had no choice other than to retrace my steps to Montgomery and go back out along the main road.

I was just about to turn around when a van drew up and a young man got out. He asked if I wanted to get through the gate because there was a key hidden down behind a rock. He fished it out, unlocked the gate for me and assured me that there would be no more locked gates to deal with. My luck had turned: the man with the van had come along just at the right moment to save me the long walk back. He relocked the gate behind me, re-hid the key and, with my thanks, drove away. Life was being good to me.

The path ahead took me along the edge of a large grass field. After about a mile we came to another gate. This one also had a chain on it. There was no lock this time, but the links of the chain had been bolted together. The bolt was too tight or too rusted to undo using fingers alone. I tried lifting it off its hinges but there was no go with that either because these had been bolted as well. After all my optimism I still had to walk all the way back again.

I am generally pretty slow to anger, but I was starting to get upset. So many times on this trip I had tried to use bridleways only to find them completely impassable. I was angry at the landowners who believe that they are entitled to block public rights of way. I walked the mile back to the other gate, only to remember that I had not bothered to watch where the nice man in the van had put the key. I fumbled around under the many rocks around the gate trying to find the one which hid the key. This part of the dyke was obviously a popular place for people to exercise their dogs. Fortunately there was lots of long grass around on which I could wipe my hands free of dog residue. After five minutes I found the right rock and the key. I felt like throwing it away and leaving the gate open – but even when angry, I am still wimpish and reasonable.

As I walked back through the park the perfect cricket pitch seemed less perfect than it had half an hour before. The birds seemed to have given up singing and started to chirp . . . monotonously. Even the sun had gone in. As I walked along I thought about how I could find out who owned the land. I planned the pithy, vituperative, incisive letter I was going to write to them. Then, just ahead of me, I saw a couple of men working on a gate. Under normal circumstances I will do anything to avoid an argument. I decided to at least ask who might be responsible for this patch of bridleway along the dyke.

135

Much to my surprise, one of the men admitted to being the local farmer and to being responsible for the land along one side of the dyke. I asked him if he knew that it was a bridleway. He said that he had been farming there for forty years and was not aware that it was.

I said that I found that extremely surprising, and asked if he thought that he was entitled to lock the gates. He said he was quite willing to tell people where the key was hidden if they had a good reason for wanting to open the gate. I replied that it would be hard for someone like me, who was just passing through, to know who to ask. I would have to be psychic to know where the key was, and to undo the other one you would need to be armed with a set of spanners. I wondered if public bridleways were only open to psychic mechanics. I am not really cut out for confrontations – I tend to go to pieces, especially when I am really dished off. The farmer said that he had to lock gates otherwise people left them open and let his stock out. I said that I was sure that they did, and that would certainly make his life difficult, but that still did not entitle him to block a public right of way.

The other man, who had been quietly listening to our conversation from behind the wheel of his pick-up truck, asked me where I was from. I was trying to decide how best to answer him when he suddenly said that in his opinion I had got a 'fucking big mouth' and that he was going to go away and come back and get me. He drove off in his truck at high speed with the gravel being kicked up behind him. I decided that I was in deep enough already. I made my excuses and left. The whole incident was very unsettling. The farmer himself had been really rather polite to me, but his friend in the pick-up truck had been rude and intimidating. I was scared that he really might come back and get me.

As it happened, I saw him and a mate parked up in a lay-by less than a mile down the road. Perhaps they had come back to put the frighteners on me. It worked, although all they actually did was to glare at Molly and me as we walked past. I tried to maintain as much dignity as I could muster, but I knew that my face was betraying my fear – just as it betrays my guilt, real or imagined, as I walk through the green channel at customs.

We had to travel along the main road for two miles before coming to a suitable lane to turn down. I stopped in the first gateway and got the map out again to see where I had been. On closer inspection, what I had taken to be a bridleway was actually classified on the map as a road used as a public path. I had been in the wrong. I felt even worse about the whole incident.

It had stayed dry since I packed up the tent, but in the afternoon David Membury's rain showers put in another unwelcome appearance. The borders seemed to be getting all the 'quite heavy' ones. The strong westerly winds aided their penetrating effect. The moisture poured in through every gap in my clothes. Molly started to look miserable as only a bedraggled horse knows how.

I had decided to join the Kerry Ridgeway which would take me eastwards into England towards Bishop's Castle. The Ridgeway is one of the few ancient routes running east to west joining England to Wales. I was not looking forward to the 600-foot climb up onto this high-level path. I was sweating profusely inside my waterproofs and was beginning to wonder what I smelt like. The road seemed unbelievably steep. Every now and again Molly would stop for a blow. I pushed on towards a spot marked as the Dog and Duck Cott, hoping against hope that it would be a pub. It wasn't.

I had assumed that it would be even windier once we joined the Kerry Ridgeway itself. Although the wind was ripping and blasting through the barley on both sides of the road, it did not feel that windy on top. The geography had taken the sting out of the wind.

About a mile outside Bishop's Castle I noticed a gypsy caravan parked in a field, just to one side of a farm drive. A tall, blonde woman was standing beside her ancient mobile home. She had her back to me and was wearing an unlikely garment for a gypsy – a short, black, plastic wet-look coat. Her bare legs were long and shapely. I thought that she must be looking at something on the ground beside the caravan, because she was hardly moving at all. As I came nearer it became

Art near Bishop's Castle – a corrugated iron boat washed up from a sea of grass.

clear that the caravan was not as it seemed. It was actually made out of old bits of scrap, mostly farm-type scrap – old cartwheels, sets of steps, shed doors and so on. The blonde woman, who had still not moved, turned out to be a shop mannikin. This was art. A few yards on I came to a large nautical tug, fifty feet long. It was made of wood and corrugated steel sheets. This also was art. It was so strange, so out of place, so confusing to the eye. It was brilliant. So brilliant that the local planning authority would prefer it not to be there.

I called in at the farm and discovered that the sculptures were made by the youngest son of a well-established borders farming family. They offered us a field to stay in down by the town. I quickly unloaded Molly, pitched the tent, threw the gear into it, and rushed off down to the shops in Bishop's Castle before they closed.

I liked the look of the town right away. It has many excellent pubs, more than could be properly sampled in a week. The streets are narrow, sloping and built on a human scale. The architecture is a comfortable mixture of everything from Elizabethan to Victorian with only a smattering of more modern buildings. The town also has proper shops – a chemist's, a newsagent's, several grocers and, best of all, a brilliant hardware shop. I needed to buy some meths for the stove and 'E. C. Davies' was the place. It is the sort of shop where there is as much stock hanging from the ceiling as litters the floor. The shop still had sledges hanging up in the window. Ron Davies, who is currently in charge, said that he was not sure whether he was hoping for the last snow of this year or looking for an early buyer for the first snow of next winter. As he spoke to me, his hand rubbed at a smooth spot on the counter. His family had been working on that smooth spot on the counter for over eighty years. The Davies family made their living by providing the community with the knackets and gadgets they needed to keep their lives running smoothly – the mantles for the lamps, the washers for taps, screws in every shape and size and material, gloves, tools, paint. It was not often that a customer came into town and failed to find what they wanted at Davies's shop. A request for meths was pretty simple to satisfy. My modest contribution towards the continuation of the Davies financial dynasty was swallowed up by the noisy till. An immense brass job it was, with ornate mouldings on the side and big numbers which jumped up at you whenever a Davies deftly pressed the finger-smoothed keys. The till was around before decimalisation. It was converted to deal with pounds and new pence. I hope it will continue to live an active and useful life – long past the time when some future member of the Davies family is forced to convert it to European Currency Units or, even worse, dollars.

But there is more to Bishop's Castle than shops, tills and pubs. It is not these which make the place world-famous. Bishop's Castle used to have a railway. The mere mention of the name will bring a smile to the face of railway buffs all over the world. Where some railways are famous for their rolling stock, the Bishop's Castle Railway was famous for being a laughing stock. For the Bishop's Castle Railway holds the world record for the longest-ever receivership. It opened in 1865, went bust in 1870 and was run by the receivers from then until 1935. That is sixty-five years. They did things differently then.

As I walked back up the high street, the town clock started striking five. A well-dressed man was emerging from the bank. I caught him just as he was locking the door. I was sure that the bank manager could tell me about the railway. He could. He was even a member of the preservation society, although there is little left to preserve save a couple of bridges and a large collection of used tickets. I explained who I was and he offered to lend me some books, provided I pushed them through the bank letter box before morning. He re-opened the bank and I followed him inside. I quizzed him some more about the railway while he was searching out the books, but he had suddenly turned rather standoffish. He started keeping his distance from me. I decided to hazard a personal question.

'Do I smell?'

'I am afraid you do, rather.'

'Horses or people?'

'An unpleasant combination of the two,' came the honest reply. Honesty is rated above politeness among bankers. Perhaps he might have been more ready to talk to me had I taken the trouble to wash before coming into town, but then I would not have got in until the shops closed. I would also have missed the bank manager. I returned to the tent where I washed and ate, and then settled down to read the first four newsletters of the Bishop's Castle Railway Society newsletter. They made great reading.

Back in 1860 the main line passed through Craven Arms – a small town some twelve miles further into England. There was a healthy social, financial and corporate rivalry between the two towns. If the people of Craven Arms had access to the nation's railway system then so too would Bishop's Castle – whatever the cost. The burghers of Bishop's Castle demonstrated considerable entrepreneurial flair combined with a poker player's willingness to take financial risks – mostly with other people's money. Their financial élan was unmatched and unsurpassed until junk-bond dealers and brewery bosses came on the financial scene over 150 years later.

Very little of the capital needed to get the Bishop's Castle Railway up and running actually came out of the pockets of the businessmen of the town. They drew up a plan with some highly optimistic figures for both costs and returns. The railway was officially opened on

26 October 1865 – about the time that the bottom fell out of the railway industry.

The railway staggered from financial crisis to financial crisis using second-hand and borrowed rolling stock, flagrantly disobeying and ignoring every safety rule and regulation in the book.

The line was far from popular with the railway establishment. On 6 January 1866 the journal the *Railway Times*, which was published continuously from 1837 to 1914, rumbled what was going on and wrote:

> This wretched abortion is submitting one of its most impudent proposals to Parliament. The preamble recites that the line between Bishop's Castle and Craven Arms is complete, which is a misapprehension of dates at all events in as much as there is neither station nor locomotive on the line. The preamble further asserts that the company are making 'considerable progress' on the remaining portion of the line between Bishop's Castle and Cambrian, which is not exactly according to fact, in as far as the term 'considerable progress' is popularly understood. The branch obtained last year from Chirbury to Minsterley remains with its ground unbroken, and yet the directors of the Bishop's Castle are not ashamed to appear in Parliament with a demand to use so much of the Cambrian as will permit the former to effect communication with the Mid-Wales, another abortion over which no one can be found to preside save Mr Whalley, and which has not yet ventured to publish a return of traffic, or to submit an account of its income and expenditure for public inspection.

You do not get many editorials to the pound like that in railway newspapers today. I am sure that the lawyers would soon be on to any newspaper which called a company a 'wretched abortion'.

In the end, even the receivers had to admit that it was a lost cause and in 1935 they finally pulled the plug on it – but by then the BCR had outlived the *Railway Times* by twenty years. There must have been at least a grain of satisfaction in that.

Chapter Thirteen

A sodden walk, a wet shave and a mad bitch called Tess

We left Bishop's Castle in pretty good condition. I had managed to have a good wash and the rain had held off enough for the tent to dry before I took it down. I intended to make a swing even further out into England down through the Clun Forest. It was an area I did not know at all and I wanted to visit Hopton Castle. As Ivor Tanner had said back in Montgomery, a castle needs to have an association with disaster and sadness for it to develop its own atmosphere. Hopton Castle was the scene of what became known as the Hopton Quarter, possibly the single most unpleasant incident of the English Civil War. Our route that day was to take us along quiet back roads through Brockton, Lower Down, Clunton and then finally to Hopton Castle – all good English-sounding names.

The day had started overcast but dry. By 11.00 a.m. it had started to rain, really rain. At first I rather enjoyed it. Molly's clip-clopping feet started plip-plopping as she walked beside me. I felt as though we were sharing the work – even though she was carrying all the gear. I started singing rain songs. It's odd how running water makes people want to sing – and convinces them that they actually sound good. Throughout the whole performance Molly plodded impassively onwards.

The Clun Forest is a beautiful place. It is a long way from being wall-to-wall trees; there are plenty of small fields scattered between the clumps. Occasionally the view opens out to expose rolling hills, but there are still enough trees around to lend form to the landscape. I like trees; they give a sense of scale to the human predicament. Man outlives nearly all his animal companions. My dog has passed from bouncing puppy to slothful old age while I have hardly changed at all. Horses live longer, but I know that some day before my fiftieth birthday I will have to face the task of calling in the knackerman to put a humane end to Molly's life. But the oak in my garden has watched humans come and go. It will be there long after I have gone.

The rain soaked through my trainers as soon as it started, and by the time I was walking down the rain-sodden road into Hopton Castle they were starting to rub and make my feet sore.

The previous day I had telephoned ahead to Hopton Castle to arrange to see a man called Peter Curnow. He lived in the village, and knew as much as anyone about the castle, its Civil War siege and the unpleasant aftermath. I arrived in Hopton Castle at about three in the afternoon and soon found Peter Curnow's house. He had managed to find a field for Molly and also offered me a bed for the night. As soon as Molly was safely grazing, Peter took me back to his cottage, thrust a cup of tea into my hand and pointed me towards the bathroom. I hope that the gesture was motivated by his sense of compassion rather than his sense of smell.

I had a lovely forty-five-minute wallow in a bath. I inspected my burgeoning collection of blisters and had a shave in real hot water. There was but one toiletry compensation to be gained from this life: I knew exactly where I was with my razors. My wife has the habit of using them on her legs. I suddenly find that my brand new razor has been turned into a high-mileage job overnight. It was not much of a compensation, I know . . .

As my trainers were so wet, I decided that I had nothing to lose, other than their bad smell, by washing them in the bath. After both I and the shoes had been cleaned, the water took on an unsavoury shade of grey.

Fortunately the rain had not penetrated my collection of plastic-wrapped bundles and I put on dry clothes and felt human again. It

143

The Curnows and their dogs offered a warm welcome at the end of a disgustingly wet day.

had stopped raining and the sun was making the occasional appearance between the black clouds. The odd burst of heat was making the lane in front of Peter's house start to steam. I went downstairs to join Peter and his wife in the kitchen. She kindly offered to park my trainers beside her range where they steamed gently.

Peter and I decided to go out and take a look at the castle while the sun was shining. With more than a twinge of regret I put my dry feet into my wet trainers and followed him out towards the castle field. He took me a couple of hundred yards down the road through the village – although Hopton Castle is now not much of a village. It has no pub, no shop and only a couple of dozen houses. Peter said that at one time it would have been much larger, but it has shrunk considerably over the past two or three centuries. We climbed a gate into a lumpy field which was covered in long lush grass. I coveted Peter's Wellington boots. In the middle of the pasture stood Hopton Castle. It was really just the tower house of a much more extensive system of fortifications, barracks and storage facilities. All the rest had gone, dismantled to make other buildings elsewhere. The sun was shining directly onto the tower but somehow it retained its dark foreboding look. The castle is a cube measuring fifty feet on each side. It is almost too perfectly ruined – more like a Victorian folly than the genuine article.

I was never that keen on history when I was at school, not having the sort of mind that can retain and regurgitate dates. But if I could have had history told to me the way that Peter Curnow told it, I would have recognised physics and chemistry for the sterile subjects they really are.

During the English Civil War this part of the borders was an almost solid Royalist area. Nearly all the surrounding landowners had sworn their loyalty to the King. Hopton, however, was owned by the Wallop family who owned several estates in Parliamentarian areas. They therefore swore allegiance to Cromwell and his crowd. The Wallops seldom visited Hopton; it was primarily an administrative centre where rents and tithes from tenants were collected. By the 1600s the castle was in the centre of quite an extensive complex of buildings, barns, houses and fortified walls. The Wallops decided to garrison the castle and instruct the thirty or so men there to hold out against the Royalists. This little bit of mischief was to cost all thirty of them their lives.

'There would have been little or nothing to gain by holding the castle here other than to waste the time and resources of the Royalists,' said Peter as we stood in the long grass of the field. 'That aside, the castle had no real strategic value. However, the Royalists could not tolerate an enemy position so deep into their own territory. They had to take it. In February 1643 they sent along a formidable force and called upon the defenders to give up. The defenders refused and an assault was attempted. It failed and large numbers of Royalists were killed.'

I was surprised that such a small number of defenders could protect such a large establishment. Peter explained that these places were well-designed to favour the defenders.

'Another famous Civil War siege took place at Corfe Castle where Lady Banks held out for a long time with the help of half a dozen men. Even Harlech Castle, which is a massive place, was held by no more than twelve men. So thirty on the inside and several hundred on the outside were pretty good odds.

'Several assaults were repulsed and eventually the Royalists returned with an even larger number of men – hundreds of them, and a number of artillery pieces as well. They were brought all the way from Ludlow, some thirty miles away, and paraded in front of the castle walls where the defenders could clearly see what they faced in the coming days.'

'Why the parade, though? Surely the attackers would prefer to keep the extent of their weaponry a secret?'

'No, no. There were strict rules about the way such affairs should be conducted. If you were defending a place and someone turned up with enough men and equipment to turf you out, they would offer quarter – that is to say, mercy. If you recognised you would be beaten, you could give up and go free without anyone being killed,' he said.

It seemed a bit like the board game of Risk.

'Exactly,' said Peter. 'That way lives on both sides are saved. However, this will only work if those being besieged give up before the battle begins. Once the first shots have been fired and lives lost, the whole thing must be allowed to run its course and the defenders face the ultimate penalty, which is death. The attackers must give no quarter for the sake of the conduct of any future sieges.

'Those inside should have known that they could not hold out indefinitely and that there was no chance of being rescued. They should have given up. For some reason, the defenders stayed with a thoroughly lost cause. The siege proper went on for several weeks,

146

with hundreds of losses on the Royalist side but only a few among the defenders. However, the Royalists had to keep going, they had to finish the job – again, for the sake of future sieges. To have started and given up halfway through could have had a disastrous effect on other sieges they might undertake.

'The guns pounded away for weeks and the defenders were slowly forced to retreat to the central part of the castle. All this is recorded by one of the defenders. They continued to fight until they heard miners working right underneath the tower. Then they knew their defence was over because the Royalists could place explosives underneath and blow the whole place apart. It was only then that they offered to lay down their arms and throw themselves on the mercy of the commander of the Royalist forces.

'They removed the barricades from the front door and came out, just in front of us here, and laid down their arms. Thirty men and two officers, I believe. The officers were marched away to billets in the

Hopton Castle, where the remorseless logic of siege warfare was played out to its bitter conclusion.

town where they were looked after by their opposite numbers on the Royalist side. The thirty men were put to the sword, every single one of them.'

It seemed terribly hard to me. Peter agreed that by today's standards it was harsh, but it is difficult for us to think ourselves into their positions.

'In my view they got what they deserved. They were summoned to surrender twice and twice they turned it down. They had held out for far longer than they should have done and had inflicted huge losses on the attackers. They had to go, had to be subjected to the full rigours of war to save more lives later.'

It still seemed terribly hard – especially since it was the officers who had made the decision not to give up and they had got off free and been taken back to sup with the Royalist officers. Peter said that was the way things were then and, to some extent, still are.

As we climbed over the gate back into the lane the castle was still bathed in bright sunlight with the dark sky behind it. It was difficult to believe that this calm quiet village had been the scene of such terrible slaughter on both sides.

That evening the Curnows took me to a pub in the next village. They had warned me beforehand that it would be an odd place. I was unprepared. From the outside, The Sun looked like an ordinary village house. Strangely enough, from the inside it looked like an ordinary house as well. The front door led into a small lobby. On the left was a tiny room with a plastic-covered trestle table running its full length. The table had three or four beer kegs on it and, clustered at the far end, a desultory collection of unused and unloved bottles of shorts and soft drinks. The Sun is not the sort of place where a stranger would feel comfortable ordering a gin and tonic.

The drinking was going on in a room to the right of the front door, an unspectacular room with a fireplace at one end, a slumbering Jack Russell curled up on the hearth, and two trestle tables with benches down each side. The central light had a terribly modest bulb in it – so modest that the flickering light from the fire in the grate picked up on the gloss-painted walls. The saloon had the feel of a British Rail waiting room on a remote country station, as though it had been kept simple so that it would be easy to clean after serious drinking sessions. The trouble was that it did not look as though anyone had bothered to take advantage of the fact. There were perhaps half a dozen people already there when we arrived. They greeted us politely and I was introduced to them all by name, including the dog, but she did not bother to interrupt her slumbers. There was just one woman in the room – an old lady perched by the door, wearing carpet slippers and a considerable number of thin beige or grey cardigans. Her hair was luxuriantly white and immaculately coiffured. She was the landlady and she asked us what we were drinking. I played safe and opted for the same as Peter. She disappeared to the other room and returned with a tray of drinks for us, and for those in the company who were lucky enough to be more than halfway through their glasses when we walked in.

The room was so small that it would have been difficult for two conversations to be carried on at once, so we all talked, or at least all listened, to tales of the recent experiences of eminent and not so eminent local people. The Jack Russell, whose name turned out to be Tess, woke up at one point and started watching invisible spiders walking around the floor. Every now and then she would bash one of them with her paw or snap at it. When she thought she had caught one of the non-existent spiders she would eat it with relish. She would then settle down for a few more minutes until the invisible spiders came and disturbed her sleep again. The conversation flowed around the room. The only time that politics or matters outside a ten-mile radius of the pub were discussed was when it was revealed that a livestock trailer had been stolen from someone's yard – 'while they slept in their beds'. This crime was blamed on people who had come from some distance away, driven to a life of crime by unemployment. Politics reared its ugly head for a few brief seconds following the use of the word unemployment, but the conversation was abruptly steered onto safer ground. A few more people came and introductions were made. The dog did a thorough job of ignoring the new recruits.

A man in the corner was persuaded to get his ukelele banjo out to lead a singsong. It was once said that the definition of a gentleman is someone who owns a ukelele but who refrains from playing it in company. Two people decided to leave, but as soon as they stood to do so, the Jack Russell leapt into action and made a growling dive for their ankles. Fortunately for them, Tess turned out to be tethered to the ukelele player's leg. She snapped and snarled at the departing people in a most inhospitable way. It took quite a while to settle her enough for the singing to start. The clock went into slow motion. As it came around to 11.00 people started to talk about leaving to go home. Tess ignored all the proceedings until she heard the word 'goodbye', and then she would enter one of her rages. Someone must have done something awful to her at one time in her life.

The beer had been good and the evening entertaining, albeit slightly bizarre. A lot of alcohol had been consumed that night. Peter told me that the pub has a very limited clientele and that sometimes the beer is awful. The landlady will never change a barrel until it is quite dry. So when a bad one is tapped the locals all pull together to drain it as quickly as possible in the hope that the next one will be better. If the barrel is good, then they will drink it more slowly to savour it and make it last. This is the stuff of a marketing man's nightmare.

Chapter Fourteen

Ley lines, a homely bookshop and a pregnant snake charmer

It should have been an easy day's walk between Hopton Castle and Knighton. Unfortunately the first half of the straightest route was through forestry land and the second half was occupied by main road. If I walked around the forest and around the main road I would not get to Knighton in one day. I had a choice: either risk losing my temper and sanity trying to get along the bridleways through the forestry land or risk losing our lives on the main road.

I decided to brave the forestry bridleways. Many of them were blocked or obscured, but it was a nice sunny day, I had slept in a bed the night before and I was mentally prepared for the frustration. I only had to trespass a few times and eventually made my way down onto a lane which ran through Bucknell, Chapel Lawn and New Invention. Now there is a name to think about.

The lane we were following narrowed slightly as it passed through a farm which had its buildings on both sides of the road. To the left was an old brick barn with windows high up on the road side. On the right were the blank sides of a modern corrugated asbestos barn. It was like walking through a rural alleyway. As we approached, the farm was strangely quiet. In retrospect it was ominously quiet, but Molly and I had been walking for three hours and neither of us was thinking very hard about our current surroundings. I had just dropped into a reverie, thinking about the meaning of the name New Invention. I have no idea what Molly was thinking about. We were

New Invention – the place where Robin Hood fitted the shoes on his horse back to front so that his enemies thought he was coming when he was going!

both brought back to reality by a ferocious barking. The alarming thing for both of us was that it came from a big black dog leaning, almost falling, out of one of the barn windows a few feet above our heads. It was so unexpected that we both jumped sideways – almost at once. I am not sure whether I was beginning to think like a horse or whether Molly was beginning to think like a human. She has a stronger personality than mine, so it is entirely possible that it might have been the former.

The dog was very, very, very upset at us. His snarl stretched back to his eyes as he leaned out of the window with one elbow hooked over the ledge. Molly and I were just beginning to realise that we were actually quite safe from the dog when his ravening and ranting was joined by another, smaller dog at the next window along. It appeared to have just as many objections to our presence – although they were not expressed with quite the eloquence and fervour of its larger companion. But, for all that, the message was well-put and clear enough:

they would both like us to jolly well go away. During the trip, Molly and I had become quite accustomed to barking dogs. We had stopped worrying about them and regarded them as part of the scenery. I had developed a theory. Actually I had been on the road long enough at this stage to believe that Molly and I had developed the theory between us. Basically, all border dogs bark and growl, but their owners are fairly sensible people. The most dangerous and genuinely vicious dogs are safely chained to their kennels. You are safe as long as you do not stray within the arc of the chain.

The other type of dogs are those which seek merely to terrorise. They lunge, teeth bared, but never actually follow through. I would growl back at them and tell them, with as much conviction and authority as I could muster, to 'Go home'. Molly would just lift one of her steel-tipped hooves in the direction of the feinted attack.

We had just passed the farm and the noise of the two dogs in the barn was dying away, when I heard a quiet growl and gentle clinking of metal on the road behind us. I felt Molly jerk her head against the leading rein and I looked behind to see yet another black dog slink-

A dog suddenly appeared at an upper window and asked us, in no uncertain terms, to go somewhere else.

ing up the road behind us. It had an unprecedented look of evil in its eye and a quiet, deep and horribly menacing growl was welling up from its throat and sinisterly slipping into the world past quivering, slavering lips. Worst of all, a ten-foot length of chain was hanging from its collar and dragging along the road behind it.

I thought to myself that if any dog was going to have us, this was the one. I heard myself saying 'Go home', but the words came out thin and hopeful rather than deep and authoritative. The dog launched itself low and hard at my heels. I was only wearing trainers and I knew that it was going to make a horrible mess. The dog was in the middle of its final approach when, wham! It did an abrupt ninety-degree change of direction in mid-lunge. The poor beast had come under the awe-inspiring influence of Molly's back leg. She had swung her foot out and around at an angle I had no idea a horse could achieve.

The dog lay inert on the verge. Remorse was just beginning to set in when the damn thing got up and came back towards us, still snarling. However, although the cur may have been thick-skinned and brave, it was not stupid. It decided to stay well out of the range of Molly's hooves. I pressed myself hard up against Molly's flank and well within the protective arc of her kick as the two of us sidled up the road followed by the grumbling dog. He followed us for over a hundred yards before turning around and walking off home. His chain made an incongruously merry chinkling noise as he went. I was pleased to see that he was limping slightly.

I felt hugely grateful to Molly. I have no illusions that her timely kick was motivated by pure self-preservation rather than any desire to protect me. However, I am still amazed at the way that she had managed to size up the situation so quickly. She had decided right away that it was no good merely threatening this dog. Direct action was called for, and she delivered it right when and where it was needed. She was amazingly accurate for a horse which has had such little practice at kicking things. I never fully regained my confidence with border dogs.

An hour later we arrived at the village of New Invention. It is a long, drawn-out place with no centre, no pub and no shop. I asked everybody I met about the name. The first person told me that it was because it was at New Invention that Robin Hood first had the idea of putting the shoes on his horse back to front. The plan was that the Sheriff of Nottingham would see the hoof prints and, assuming that Robin Hood was coming when he was going and going when he was coming, give chase in entirely the wrong direction. He would soon arrive at a place which Robin had just left. It was a good story, but we were a long way from Sherwood or Nottingham. I received a couple more suggestions, but they were mere variations on a theme and had either Dick Turpin or Caractacus in the starring role.

Then a farmer in a Land Rover stopped to admire Molly and to ask where I was headed. We spoke for a while about horses and travelling. Then I asked him about New Invention. He told me, with some authority, that it stemmed from the invention of a water-driven wool-carding machine which was built there in the sixteenth century. It was much less exciting than the horseshoe idea, but much more credible – thereby demonstrating that fact is usually much more boring than fiction.

I had been told that if there is one section of the Offa's Dyke path that I ought to walk then the bit between Knighton and Kington was it. It rolls up and down through wonderful countryside as it crosses a small cluster of hills. As it winds south you can see the path and the Dyke stretching away in front, dipping in and out of sight as it switchbacks through the hills and valleys. It is a shame that it is just a footpath and that the number of stiles between Kington and Knighton makes it totally impossible for a horse to get along it. I had to take Molly the long way around along the top of a ridge on the English side of the Dyke and path.

It began as a nice walk, but the temperature started to climb and the flies came out. They did not bother me much but the horseflies went straight for Molly. I had always assumed that horses used their tails to brush flies away, but Molly was swishing hers viciously at them. She caught me around the side of the face with one of her more aggressive swipes. It hurt and left quite a welt on my face. A well-aimed swish of a horse tail must be lethal for flies. The flies on her front end caused more problems. She could vibrate her skin to make it difficult for them to settle, but once they were attached and sucking blood there was little she could do. She would then start bashing me in the back with her head and eventually stop dead in the road, refusing to budge until I had located the horsefly and ruined its day by swatting it with my hand. A small red splodge with a squashed fly in the middle would be left on her fur, but I felt no remorse.

I stopped in Presteigne and bought some fly repellent for Molly. It made her smell awful, partly because of the chemicals, but mainly because the manufacturers try and cover up the bad odour with a perfume – a cheap perfume. Possibly one that was rejected even by the Brut factory.

It was at about three in the afternoon that she started to rattle. Nothing serious at first, just the faintest hint of a metallic clink every time she put her back nearside foot down. By five o'clock, as I was coming into Kington, the shoe was so loose that I could see it move as she walked. We would not be going much further without the services of a blacksmith.

I found a very nice place to stay just outside Kington. I saw to Molly's immediate needs, pitched the tent and walked back into town. Kington turned out to be a compact, attractive little place, but I had more pressing business.

There are three things required for complete satisfaction in a public toilet – a seat, toilet paper and a lock on the door. Municipal authorities only ever supply two out of three. Kington was no exception.

I then spent a fruitless hour on the telephone failing to get a farrier. I tried bribing them with double their normal fee, but none of them was able to help me inside of a week. Like many other people who have dealt with horses, I live in fear of farriers. They have you under their complete control. They are worse than dentists. They like you to book regular check-ups for maintenance rather than waiting until something goes wrong. They make more money that way. They also hate their clients shopping around. If you take a horse to a new farrier he will pick up its feet, offer a long intake of breath, suck his teeth a little and then ask, 'Who did this last time, then?' – the implication being that you must have employed a cowboy and the soundness of your horse has been placed severely at risk. Give me a visit to the dentist any time.

I went back to the farm where we were staying. The farmer was out checking his cattle and I told him about Molly's rattling shoe and my fruitless search for a farrier. He disappeared into the house, and came back a few minutes later to tell me that someone would be coming over the following evening to do Molly's shoes. Some people have no fear.

That solved one problem, but left me with another. I would have a whole day to spend in Kington which is not a very big town. Ian, my temporary landlord, suggested that I go up to the church to see the tomb of Black Vaughan and Ellen the Terrible. I had doubts whether I could make the visit last all day, but if that was all Kington had to offer, then I would give it a try.

In the morning I headed up towards Kington Church, which is perched on a hill overlooking the town. I walked in through the porch just as the clock was striking ten. In a side chapel, there is a large, raised tomb with the supine statues of two bodies, Black Vaughan and Ellen the Terrible. Well, that was exciting. The clock had hardly stopped chiming ten by the time I re-emerged. I had done Kington in slightly less than two minutes.

I sat on a seat in the graveyard and contemplated the empty hours stretching away before me. A shadow fell across me and I looked up to see a man walking slowly past clutching two bent bits of coat hanger. He walked on around the corner. Odd, I thought. I wondered what else I could do that day. Buy a book? I had just got on to trying to decide whether to buy something which would improve my mind or something entertaining, when the man with the coat hangers came past again. He must have done a complete circuit of the church. He was a big man, with black hair and an impressive Mexican-style moustache.

I had just decided to buy some rubbish to read and spend the day lounging around the tent when he came past for the third time. I could bear it no more. I stood up and followed him at a respectful distance as he made his fourth circumnavigation. Occasionally, the two bits of coat hanger would move towards each other. He would stop, get out a notebook and a compass and write down a bearing. Finally he stopped by a gravestone, spread a map out and started drawing lines across it.

Then I ambled up and, as casually as I could, asked him what he was doing.

'Looking for ley lines,' he said, as calmly as if he had told me he was waiting for the next number nineteen bus. He was looking for features on the map which might tie in with their compass bearings. He showed me where one was supposed to run, pointing out a series of hill forts, churches or clumps of trees which, he said, were proof of its existence and relevance. Draw a line at random on a map of the borders and there is a good chance that it will run through a church or a fort or a clump of trees every now and again. I asked Keith what was so special about Kington Church.

'All sorts of things,' he said. He told me that the church had a very strange and powerful atmosphere. I have to admit that I had not felt a thing a few minutes before when I had gone in alone. But when Keith took me back in there and led me over to the statues of Black Vaughan and his wife and then started telling me, in a hushed voice, about the legends surrounding these two and their tomb, I began to feel uneasy. Black Vaughan is supposed to come back once every 100 years in the shape of a black animal. Once it was as a big black bull, another time it was as a big black dog which terrorised the area. Conan Doyle wrote *The Hound of the Baskervilles* while staying just up the road at Clyro. Keith told me about a woman who had seen a giant black bull in the church; he pointed down at a cracked flagstone at our feet and said that was the result of the bull's visit. Flower arrangements in the church are supposed to reorganise themselves in the shape of a bull's head.

Keith then persuaded me to get down on my hands and knees to examine some stains on the bottom of the Vaughan tomb. He said that these stains were exactly the same as bloodstains on stone. They had suddenly appeared some years before. Rubbish of course, but when delivered in a silent church in a quiet, serious voice by a man with two bits of bent coat hanger sticking out of his top pocket, such stories can make one feel slightly uncomfortable. I was pleased to leave the church.

Keith turned out to be a psychic investigator, author and mini-cab driver. The cab was his main source of income. I learnt a lot about him and his view of the world in the following hour. He loves Lea and Perrins sauce, but hates homogenised roadside eating places – one chain he dubbed 'the Puking Pacman'. In his view, Sir Edward Elgar wrote brilliant music but should have left the librettos to someone else. He mourns the impending demise of the old-style phone kiosks: 'If we repent as a nation, perhaps we shall be blessed with the return of our original boxes,' he said.

Keith also had some interesting perspectives on history. Take the Romans: 'A nation of jobsworths. The rules said that a Roman fort had to have four doors, one for each major point of the compass. Roman fort builders put in the four doors, even if the fort was right on the edge of a cliff and one step through the entrance would offer nothing more than a downward trip to oblivion.'

He also offered a theory for the two-fingered salute, which ought to be true even if it is not. According to Keith, the French knights recognised that the English bowmen (Welsh actually, he said) represented a considerable military threat. The French promised that any Englishman taken prisoner would never draw a bow again: they intended to remove both the index and middle finger on the right hand of every prisoner. Of course, the French lost the battle of Agincourt, and it became the habit among the British soldiery to

Arrow Books was supposed to be
a shop, but Bob Jenkins loved the books too much to part with them.

hold up their two fingers to any French military personnel they might come across. The gesture was found to be so satisfying for the donor, and so annoying for the recipient, that it continues today as a traditional greeting between our nations.

Keith told me that toll dodging was a favourite Welsh pastime. They would leave the toll road just before coming to a booth, walk up into the hills to one side and then come back down onto the road once they had passed the booth. The idea was to stay out of sight of the toll house the whole way. He told me to look on the map at the location of any toll booth and you will still see public rights of way marked as going around the booths. I cannot vouch for the veracity of the rest of Keith's stories but a quick scan of my maps back at the tent proved that this, at least, was true.

After I had watched Keith pack away his divining coat hangers into the back of his mini-cab and said goodbye to him, I walked back down into town. Somehow I felt that I wanted to know more about Ellen the Terrible and Black Vaughan. They must have been awful people to earn their names, but not so awful that they were not allowed to be buried in the church. That is a pretty fine line to tread. I asked around town and was pointed in the direction of one of Kington's two bookshops. Arrow Books turned out to be low and dark and old. Posters advertising local events, some of which had happened weeks ago, were stuck in the windows, making the interior even darker than the long-dead architect intended. I tried the door. It was locked. I peered in, cupping my hands around my face to exclude the bright light outside. There were racks and stacks of second-hand books. I was just about to give up when a lady came up and asked if I was looking for Mr Jenkins. I said that I supposed that I was, so she offered to go around the back and knock him up. It seemed a strange way to run a bookselling business, but Mr Jenkins was not really all that interested in selling books. After a few minutes I heard the lock on the door slide back and the door was pulled back to reveal Bob Jenkins. He was small, white-haired, over sixty, over-weight and inordinately pleased to see me.

I asked him if he could tell me about Black Vaughan and his charming wife, Ellen the Terrible. Lesser men might have been thrown by such a request from a complete stranger. Bob invited me in. I had to duck to get through the door. The shop smelled of books that had been sitting on shelves for a long time. As my eyes adjusted to the poor light I saw that Arrow Books had a lived-in look to it – the odd coffee cup, a comfortable chair, a pile of papers. Bob, for we were already on first-name terms, invited me through to the kitchen. The piles of books and papers had started to grow there as well.

There was no clear dividing line between where the bookshop stopped and the living part of the house began. The two functions blended comfortably and seamlessly into each other.

Bob settled me down in his kitchen and offered me whisky or tea, or both. It had only just gone eleven. I had tea, he had whisky. Black Vaughan was a bit of a disappointment. He turned out to be no more than a local landowner who got his name from the colour of his hair and who lost his life at the battle of Banbury in 1469.

But what of Ellen the Terrible?

'There is a bit more to her – she made a famous revenge attack. One of her kinsmen, a cousin I believe, was murdered. She bided her time until an archery contest was being held at which the murderer was to take part. Ellen dressed herself in men's clothing and entered the competition. Just as it came to her turn to shoot at the target, she swung her bow around and finished off the murderer. A vengeful and resourceful woman.'

I asked him how long she outlived her husband. It was only an idle question, but Bob said that he could tell me exactly how long she had been in charge of the estates. He went over to one of his impressive piles of paper and started raking through it. He failed to find what he was after and led me through to another room and another pile of paper. Bob Jenkins subscribed to the deep-litter system of filing.

Half an hour later he had failed to find the piece of paper with the dates on it, but he had turned up several other things – among them a poem written by Kington's most famous poet, Christopher Harvey:

'Tis dinner time, and now I look for a full meal
God has sent me a good cook.
This is the dresser board
And here I wait in expectation of good cheer.
I am sure the master of the house,
enough to entertain his guests allows.
And not enough of some one sort alone,
But choice of what best fitteth every one.

Bob waited for me to say what a nice poem it was. I could not disappoint him so I lied. He read out a lot more examples of Christopher Harvey's work in the belief that he had found a kindred spirit. Harvey's poetry was an acquired taste – a taste I feared I never would acquire. I stayed until two, heard a lot more of Harvey's hideous doggerel, but never did find out how long Ellen outlived Vaughan.

I bought a local paper and spent the remains of the afternoon in the tent waiting for the farrier to turn up. The paper said that

Mr Jolly's Circus was in town and that it was auditioning for a new snake charmer because the present incumbent had fallen pregnant. How could I not go?

As soon as the farrier had finished I headed off back to town. I almost ran, because I had not booked a seat and was worried that I would not get in. I need not have bothered; there was no queue. Turning people away was something Mr Jolly dreamed about the way other people dream of winning the football pools.

Mr Jolly had found a perfect pitch for his circus on the edge of the recreation ground down near the river. His big top was not all that big – but it was the right shape and colour with red, white and blue panels in the roof. I was almost alone as I approached a caravan bearing the legend 'Mr Jolly's Ticket Office'. Feeling terribly self-conscious and foolish, I bought a ticket.

The inside of the big top seemed to be completely dark. My eyes adjusted to the gloom. The top seemed huge – but then I had been living in a six-foot by four-foot tent for a month. The ring in the middle was about forty feet across. There was no sawdust, just the grass of the recreation ground. There was no smell of greasepaint, just

Mr Jolly, less than happy about his modest audience figures.

the sweet, oily smell of a generator. There were banks of seats – probably enough for 300 people. I counted the audience. It did not take long: thirteen of us – five adults and eight children. I wondered how long Mr Jolly could stay in business if all he managed to pull were audiences of thirteen. The ticket sales of £18 would barely cover the fuel costs of the generator thrumming away outside. The few remaining minutes to five o'clock ticked away. One more adult and two children came blinking into the tent.

Suddenly the lights went down, the floodlights went up and that well-known circus music started: dan, dan, daddle, daddledan, dan, daan, dan. Only it missed that bit out and started somewhere in the diddle of the eighth bar, as though a cassette had not been wound right back. It hadn't.

As suddenly as it had started, the music cut out and a distorted voice came over the Tannoy: 'Ladies and gentlemen, boys and girls, welcome to Mr Jolly's family circus.' The music burst back in. Then it went again.

'So, without more ado,' said the tinny Tannoy voice, 'let's get the show on the road with Mr Jolly and the proud performing horses.' The music started again – a different tune this time, but rendered familiar by the same organ playing it. Two diminutive ponies rushed into the ring. They looked in pretty good condition but were wearing those horrible circus harnesses which are designed to put a graceful curve in their necks and make them prance prettily. The trouble is that the tightly reigned-in bit also makes the horse grimace as it moves around the ring.

A big man with unnaturally black hair and wearing a bright red jacket walked into the ring, carrying a whip and three stones too much weight. On command the ponies ran around the ring, turned around, jumped over a stick, and reared up on their hind legs. They did all the standard circus manœuvres. Every now and again the music would suddenly change as though the new song had been recorded over the top of the previous one.

The ponies finished their act and left the ring, followed by Mr Jolly and a terribly modest round of applause.

Then it was Caroletta and her performing poodles. The woman who came into the ring was aged about forty – a reasonably good-looking forty. She had unnaturally black hair which was permed to fall about her shoulders. She gave the impression of having a lot of teeth and was wearing too much make-up. She had once had a good figure and almost still did. The poodles did all the things performing poodles do. They jumped through hoops, they did backward somer-saults from a standing start, they climbed ladders. There was one larger poodle which was supposed to push its fellow poodles in a pram but it clearly found the whole thing far too exciting. The kids beside and behind me thought it was terribly entertaining.

As soon as Caroletta had disappeared through the curtain, the music cut out. 'Ladies 'n' gen'l'men, boyz 'n' girlz, Bashir the Bactrian camel.' Up came a Middle-Eastern style tune performed on the Ham-mond organ – rendering it bizarre to people from both sides of the Mediterranean. A rather sad-looking camel came in, followed closely by Mr Jolly and his whip. Bashir looked suitably imperious but was forced to put his front feet up on a giant metal stool. His feet were too close to the edge and the stool flipped over giving him a nasty crack on the shins. I winced and looked at the faces of the other members of the audience. The adults were impassive, the children enraptured by the whole thing.

Then came a balancing act: 'Ladies 'n' gent'l'men, boyz 'n' girlz, introducin' Mary-Anne and Julie-Anne.' Two awkwardly adolescent girls came into the ring, each standing on a large, three-foot diameter ball and rolling it with her feet. The girls were wearing sparkling leotards which were cut inappropriately high on the thigh for such young children. Their gawky smiles revealed large numbers of teeth as they gingerly rolled their balls around the ring and up and down slopes.

Other acts followed. The costumes and the routines were differ-ent but the performers were somehow familiar. Throughout it all the rickety tape recorder wowed and crackled its way through a repertoire of familiar tunes: 'The Good, the Bad and the Ugly', 'Guantanamera', 'Do Not Forsake Me Oh My Darling'. Eventually the interval came.

During the second half we had Caroletta with her performing pigeons. One of the males appeared to be more interested in sex than the sort of performance Caroletta had in mind for him. The clowns did some more routines with lots of 'Look out behind you' and 'Oh yes we did'. One of the girls went up on a high wire. Mr Jolly walked anxiously underneath, ready to catch her should she fall. Her wobbles looked genuine. Towards the end there was an act called P.J. Junior and the Westernettes. Young Peter Jolly twirled a rope, cracked a bullwhip, fired guns and threw knives at his mother. Until the knife-throwing, Caroletta's toothy smile had been unwavering and even looked genuine at times. Wearing a red fringed miniskirt, which showed ten inches more thigh than I really wanted to see on a woman her age, Caroletta cowered against the left-hand edge of an old door while her son threw knives into the right-hand side. One of the knives came too close for my peace of mind. Caroletta's smile looked even less authentic. Then she tried to move across to the other edge of the door to leave plenty of room for P.J. Junior to throw his remaining knives. The knife which had come too close for comfort was stopping her from moving very far. She pulled it out and shuffled to the right leaving enough room for P.J. to complete the act successfully without harming her.

Then, still on a Western theme, in came Indian Joe. 'And remember, boyz 'n' girlz, we do ask that you don't try this at home otherwise you could get seriously hurt.' I wondered what Indian Joe was going to do which required this stern warning if throwing knives at mother did not. Indian Joe was a fire-eater. He was good at it too. He also turned out to be the snake charmer. Indian Joe did not look pregnant.

I found Mr Jolly outside tinkering with one of his lorries. He seemed quite happy to talk. So, had it been a successful show for him?

'Yes, yes I think so. Financially a disaster, but the audience seemed to enjoy it and if only a few of them turn up then we owe it to them to put one on,' said Mr Jolly in a voice which did not live up to his name. The blame for the small audience he laid firmly at the door of King Orry, whose circus had just started using the same route. It was being run by a former employee of Mr Jolly and he was using Mr Jolly's good name to get the sites. Malicious rumours had been spread about the demise of Mr Jolly's circus. As for the pregnant snake charmer, Mr Jolly conceded that it might have been a bit of a wind-up. Made a change from the old story about looking for a new lion tamer. It is a hard one to use if the circus has no lions anyway.

Chapter Fifteen

Hang-gliders, Hergest Ridge and heavy metal monks

As I walked through Kington town centre at 9.30 in the morning, it was already busy. The clatter from Molly's new shoes echoed off the buildings on either side of the narrow high street. Her feet, freshly trimmed by the farrier, looked neat and square, like well-manicured fingernails. That morning I had spent an extra ten minutes with the grooming brush. She looked neat and tidy. The main street was quite congested with buses, cars and tractors. Vehicles stopped to let us through the narrow bits where cars had been thoughtlessly parked. I saw Mrs Jolly and her son Peter lugging a huge amount of shopping back towards the recreation ground where the circus tent was pitched. A street sweeper was tidying up the main square. To my eyes, accustomed to London litter, the job did not need doing. He was sweeping up dust rather than litter.

We walked up the hill past the church where Black Vaughan and Ellen the Terrible were sleeping peacefully, and headed out of town along the bridleway towards Hergest Ridge. It is a long hill, sticking out 1000 feet above the surrounding countryside.

The bridleway onto the Ridge starts as a metalled lane passing up through an area of increasingly expensive houses with increasingly leafy gardens, one of which is open to the public every day between ten and six. Then the road is blocked by a nice five-barred gate with a neatly spliced piece of green rope holding it closed. There were a few cars parked around the gateway while their owners took advantage of the dry day to exercise their dogs and their legs on the Ridge.

I met an elderly man and a young woman coming down off the Ridge, both carrying sizeable rucksacks. They were father and daughter, walking the Dyke together. Just the two of them, stealing a few days together away from their families. The man's wife was looking after his daughter's family, having a great time playing mother to a brood of three. The father and daughter were getting to know each other again. They carried on down into Kington, I went on up through the gate and onto Hergest Ridge. My son is only two years old. I hoped that he would be prepared to walk with his father in twenty years' time. I felt slightly lonely.

Through the gate, the trees retreated from the path, leaving it as a flattened strip of grass running across a wide area of common land. My melancholy did not last long. I remembered that it was ten o'clock on a Wednesday morning and that I was having a much better time now than I would have had at work. Molly's feet clomped gently on the turf. It made a change from the precise clip-clop of hooves on tarmac or grinding on gravel. The sun was shining, but there were enough clouds around to keep the sky interesting. The path started to get steeper, but I was getting fit and I had not done much walking the day before. It was lovely to be out in the fresh air, walking in such a beautiful place. The map marked a racecourse up on top of the Ridge. It could just be made out as a ring of flatter ground, more oval-shaped than round. It did not look as though it had been used for horses much, although a few four-wheel-drive nutters had obviously been racing around it.

Further up towards the summit, there is a cluster of rocks where I sat for a few minutes while Molly cropped the short turf around us. The skylarks were singing above us and the occasional insect flew past, but there was something else, a constant noise which never let up. I am sure that a month before I would never have noticed it, but now it was an annoying background, waxing and waning, but always there. It was the sound of engines – sometimes lorries, sometimes motorbikes, high-flying jets or low-flying piston aeroplanes. It was

Hergest Ridge, where we spent four hours wandering around in circles getting nowhere at all.

the sound of people travelling. Back at the beginning of the journey there had been times when I had heard nothing other than the natural sounds of the countryside. Now I was back to that buzz of civilisation. If I needed a reminder that I was coming towards the end of the journey, this was it.

Hergest Ridge is a sort of lozenge shape, four miles long and 1000 feet high. The top is not clearly defined, nor is the path that goes up and over it. Coming down the other side was almost a mirror image of going up. The trees started to close in towards the path and there was another five-barred gate with a piece of green cord on it. A few cars were parked on the other side; obviously people walked onto the Ridge from both ends. The lane looked pretty much the same as the one at the other end as well. Then I came to a sign telling me that one of the gardens was open to the public between ten and six. It is the first time that I have felt schizophrenic. Two parts of my brain were having an argument with each other and I could not decide which side to join. One side was arguing quite rationally that it was entirely possible for the paths on either side of Hergest Ridge to be almost the same. The other side was accusing me of being an idiot for having been up on the hill, having turned around through 180 degrees without knowing it and having come back down the same way I had gone up. Three hours had gone down the tubes. Then Molly's pack slipped and I spent the next ten minutes sorting that out.

I considered walking up along the Ridge all over again, but thought better of it and chose a shorter route leading along the back lanes towards Hay-on-Wye. It should have been an easy day's walk, but I had mentally spoilt it by my three-hour detour. Every time I looked at the map to see where I was I could not stop myself from looking six miles up the road to see where I would have been.

The route took me across the River Wye at a toll bridge. It is owned by a family who saw it advertised in the paper, came to see it for a laugh and then decided to go ahead and buy it. The lady let me through for nothing because she said that Molly was the first packhorse to use the bridge since her family had bought it, and besides, she did not know how much to charge me.

The remaining four miles to Hay-on-Wye were along the fertile flood plain of the River Wye. We passed close to Clifford Castle, which was once the home of a young aristocratic wench called Rosamund – as in fair Rosamund. She was unlucky enough to have caught the eye of Henry II and greatly upset Eleanor, Henry's wife. Tennyson wrote a verse or two about Rosamund and what she was doing to upset Queen Eleanor:

> 'Turn around and look on me:
> I am that Rosamond, whom men call fair,
>   If what I was I be.
> 'Would I had been some maiden coarse and poor!
>   Oh me, that I should ever see the light!
> Those dragon eyes of anger'd Eleanor
>   Do hunt me, day and night.'

I arrived at Hay-on-Wye around seven in the evening. Had it not been for my Hergest detour it would have been four in the afternoon. I had started the day rejoicing at how fit I was getting and finished it completely exhausted.

171

I was looking forward to the next section of my journey which was to take us through the Black Mountains. As mountains go, they are a bit of a disappointment. They are really no more than a cluster of vegetation-covered ridges rising to a pretty modest 800 metres. They are terribly frustrating to climb because their curved tops offer the walker a series of false summits. You see ahead what must surely be the top, only to find another summit above that. Again and again the visual trick is played, until you find yourself on the flattened, peat-boggy top of the mountain. The actual summit may be hundreds of yards away from the edge and offer little more than extensive views of other, equally uninteresting, round-topped mountains – assuming that you have chosen one of the few clear days. The Black Mountains look more dramatic when viewed from the valleys below than from the ridges above.

Fortunately love is blind and, for all their faults, I have always had a soft spot for these mountains and the people who live there. When I think of Wales I think of the Llanthony Valley and the mountains which run along either side of it. As I walked away from Hay-on-Wye I had a feeling of coming home. For the first time, I could leave the map in the pack because I knew the area well.

The road up from Hay-on-Wye follows the border – or maybe the border follows the road. It does not really matter which. It rises steeply around gear-crunching bends, through Cusop Dingle and eventually across a cattle-grid marking the start of Hay Common. Suddenly the exuberant hedgerows on either side disappear, to be replaced by grass verges which have been cropped unbelievably short by the sheep and wild ponies. And where there are wild ponies, there are likely to be wild stallions. I armed myself with a stick and a pocketful of pebbles just in case I needed to defend Molly's honour. The trouble was that I knew that, should push come to shove and she managed to attract the attention of any passing stallion, then Molly would be doing her best to lose her honour. A stick and a pocketful of pebbles did not seem to be much of a defence against half a tonne of equine passion, but I would do my best to ensure that Molly finished the trip *virgo intacta* – assuming that she still was.

The road levelled out across the common where a few picnickers had stopped for lunch beside their cars. A few hang-gliders were floating above the common on the wind which was blowing in from the northwest. The road started to get steep again as it headed up towards the Gospel Pass. It got so narrow that there was only room for one car. Oncoming vehicles had to stop to let us walk past. Cars coming from behind had to stop to allow me to turn Molly around to face them as they edged past us.

I stopped at the top of the Gospel Pass and looked over the Golden Valley of the River Dore. It certainly looked fertile compared to the sloping, thinly-grassed land around me. The Welsh inhabitants of the Black Mountains must have looked enviously at the territory taken over by the English incomers. This spot was named the Gospel Pass because St Peter was supposed to have stood here and decided to found a church in the valley below. There is a village there called Peterchurch.

There is something unique about the character of the people who inhabit these mountains. There has always been a lot of religion in the Black Mountains; and the churches, and the way they have been treated, say a lot about the people here. A few miles south of Lord Hereford's Knob there is a village called Partrishow. It has a rather conventional, stone-built church, but it is the inside which is so extraordinary. The walls of the church have been whitewashed for

A bizarre decoration for the back wall of a church – worth wondering what sort of fourteenth-century vicar would have commissioned such a work of art.

many years. During one cleaning session an extremely ugly figure of a skeleton started to emerge on the rear wall of the church. It had been painted life-size, or possibly slightly larger, and was carrying an hourglass, a scythe and a spade – clearly an uncaped grim reaper. The interior of the church is frequently repainted with emulsion, all except for a square around the figure which has been left the original dull grey colour. It makes the image even more threatening, as though it has somehow managed to open up a doorway to hell in the back wall of the church and is coming forward to claim its victims. The presence of such a figure on the rear wall of a church must say something about the people of the area – and the sort of clergy they employ.

Other Black Mountain churches reveal a lot about the frontier nature of the place. When the people here heard of the Wars of the Roses, they naturally assumed that any day a group of protagonists from one side or the other might come thundering through, generally disturbing the peace and burning things. The interior of the church at Llanelieu is decorated with both red and white roses painted on the walls. The plan was to find out who it was who was doing the burning, the Yorkists or the Lancastrians, and to nip into the church to paint out the offending set of roses. That way, whichever faction came through, the church would be left unburnt. As it happened, the Wars of the Roses was one of the few disputes to have broken out in Britain which left this area untouched.

With that cheerful thought in mind I stood up and started walking south down the Llanthony Valley. Before leaving the common land I did come across a group of wild ponies. Molly looked expectantly in their direction. I hefted the stick in my hand but they were all mares, pot-bellied and heavily in foal. They left us alone.

Two hours later I was in the village of Capel-y-ffin, if you can call one house, one phone box and one chapel a village. I went on up to The Grange, which is now used as a pony-trekking centre, and asked if I could turn Molly into one of their fields for the night. The owner, Dai Griffiths, was worried that Molly might be carrying equine 'flu, which produces the same symptoms in horses as human 'flu produces in people – coughing, wheezing and generally feeling rotten. It is almost never fatal, but it can put a horse out of work for six weeks or more. It could sweep through the forty horses at The Grange in a matter of days; Dai would have to deal with some very disappointed holiday-makers and an extremely disappointed bank manager. He was reassured when I told him that Molly had received her jabs before the trip and had not shared a field with another horse since I had taken Kate and the foal home.

Dai asked if he could come out and see Molly. I was a bit surprised at his request because I knew that he was completely blind. One of his daughters led him out into the yard where he ran his hands over her. He felt her all over, up and down her legs, her head, her ears, across her back. He guessed that she had some Suffolk in her. He had only been blind for five years, but people who really know horses have always relied on the evidence of their hands as much as their eyes. He even offered me a price for her – it was outrageously low, but what can you expect from someone who knows horses?

Dai had lived in the valley since the fifties and had been running a trekking centre almost as long. He had lost his sight in an operation about five years before. He was still very much in control of his business, although the day-to-day running of the trekking centre was now being handled by his two daughters. The Grange offers pony-trekking holidays all through the summer. Since Dai's illness, they have started offering treks for visually handicapped people. A party of them had been booked in for the next day and Dai said that Molly and I were welcome to join them. I could even make myself useful by following up the rear to pick up any dropped hats and to close the gates after them. I then took Molly down to a field by the village where Dai said that we could stay, and bedded down for the night.

About ten o'clock a number of cars and minibuses turned up at The Grange and a variety of people dressed ready for riding got out. A few wore proper riding boots, most wore stout shoes. One particularly noisy group of kids were clustered around the back of their minibus waiting for their packed lunches to be handed out. They had sandwiches, real sandwiches with real bread. I thought of my forth-coming lunch of dried fruit, nuts and Garibaldi biscuits. It was not until I noticed one of the children being guided towards the toilet that I realised that this was the party of blind kids. There were eight or nine pupils from a special college and almost as many helpers. Their group leader was a much adored Miss Ray, whose name rang out around the yard as the kids competed for her atten-tion and her affection. I went up and introduced myself to her and said that I would be recording at times during the day. Suddenly I was surrounded by the kids who were saying very nice things about BBC Radio, asking very knowledgeable questions about my tape recorder and requesting to feel both it and the microphone.

One of Dai's daughters allocated the ponies according to the size and experience of the riders. The kids were led over to them, told what colour their horses were, given a brush each and then told to get on with it. There was a lot of noise, but you cannot expect a group of blind kids to be quiet. The kids were then called back to the tack room and given the saddles to match their ponies. Within half an hour we were away.

It was pretty much the same as going out with any group of pony trekkers, except there were a lot more shouted warnings about low trees and steep banks. Actually there was a lot more shouting all round. They had several in-words, just like kids at any other school. 'Ah-lads' appeared to be a general buzz word, 'soz' was used instead of 'sorry' and the highly dubious 'tollocks' was thrown around with abandon.

There was another difference between this and ordinary treks. When I worked at a trekking centre in the holidays, a major part of my job as backstop was to get off and pick up hats and other bits of clothing which the trekkers had dropped. Blind people take great care not to drop or lose things. Finding them again is very time-consuming when you can only feel.

Most of the children had been taught the basics of horse riding at a proper riding school. They all knew how to get on and off horses, how to stop them and how to make them go faster. The kids preferred pony trekking to ordinary riding lessons because they liked the open spaces and the idea of travelling somewhere on a horse rather than just going round and round in circles. One said that although he could not see the mountains, he could 'feel' them. As I rode along at the back I closed my eyes and tried to 'feel' the mountains. I remembered them, could conjure up an image of them as they looked just before I closed my eyes, but I cannot say that I could 'feel' them.

After two or three hours' riding we stopped for lunch in a clearing in an area of planted forestry. The kids started pumping me about my trip and about Molly. One of the girls asked if she could go and see Molly. The kids used the word 'see' even if what they meant was 'feel'. I took her over to where Molly was tied up and Lychanne ran her hands over Molly's head, neck and legs. She did not say much at the time, but when she rejoined the main group Lychanne started telling them about Molly's massive build, her weird haircut and about my strange saddle and stirrups. I had not even noticed her feeling the saddle. Lychanne could 'see' more with her hands than most people can see with their eyes.

I also managed to swop some of my rotten old Garibaldi biscuits for sandwiches. I got a lot from those kids.

The next morning Molly and I walked down the valley road. With each passing mile the flood plain got wider and more fertile, the fields and the trees got larger. The terrain changed incredibly fast over the eight miles from the Gospel Pass to Llanthony Priory which stands in the sort of scenery which Constable would have been happy to paint – in the summer, anyway. I stopped at the priory for lunch, partly because I like the place, but mostly because it has a bar in its cellars. The bar is now only open at lunchtimes following an incident several years ago when a gang of Hell's Angels took over the place. The priory has long been the focus of various types of border insanity – mostly inflicted on it by outsiders. Llanthony Priory is now pretty much a ruin, but enough of it remains to give an idea of its former scale and glory. Although that may be misleading: instead of just a vaulted roof, the walls now support the sky; and the views of the valley, which the vacant window arches now frame, must surely be more impressive than the stained-glass contrivances of man which once filled them. So perhaps the place is more impressive as a ruin than it was in its prime in the thirteenth century.

St David, the patron saint of Wales, was supposed to have built a cell at Llanthony. Six hundred years later, a lost Norman knight called William de Lacy stumbled on the place. He decided to give up his life of hunting, killing and debauching and take up a life of religious contemplation.

Unfortunately, merely sitting having a good time looking at the scenery and thinking good thoughts would not have fitted in with the Norman work ethic: there had to be a bit of suffering as well. William decided that he would make his life harder by keeping his suit of armour on all the time. The weight and the chill metal would keep him in line. However, Wales is a wet place. The armour started rusting badly. As each bit dropped off he replaced it with an equivalent weight of scrap metal. This man was clearly in need of a psychoanalyst. All this suffering and virtue went down really well with William's fellow Normans. Lots of people turned up to join William's life of religious contemplation.

The Church wanted to regularise things so they sent in a few proper monks from Colchester and London and a pukka religious community formed.

By 1120 there were forty monks at Llanthony. They were known as the Black Canons because of their black robes. All went well for fifteen years until Llanthony became the centre of a bizarre incident in which a Welsh bandit (or prince, depending on which side you are backing) claimed sanctuary at the priory along with fifty men.

The Norman pursuers, who may have been regretting ever allowing Llanthony to become a proper religious community, could do nothing other than join in the wait outside the main church. The stalemate dragged on for months. The poor old Black Canons tried to carry on their lives as normal – not an easy thing to do with heavily-armed men lounging around both sides of the church door. Eventually the Bishop of Hereford, who was a bit of a softy and an ex-Llanthony inmate, took pity on the Black Canons. He invited them to come over to Hereford to stay and pray while the opposing armies got on with it. The Black Canons liked it there so much that they refused to go back to Llanthony even though the armed men had given up and gone home. The priory appears to have become a sort of reform school for bad monks or, as one contemporary writer put it:

> The monastery was reduced to such straits that the inmates had no surplices – sometimes no breeches – and could not with decency attend divine service.
>
> The monks at the daughter church at Gloucester were revelling in abundance and wealth. They even made sport of our woes and when one was sent here would ask what fault he had committed. Thus it was that the Mistress and mother house was called a dungeon and place of banishment to men as if guilty of every crime.

The whole place folded towards the end of the fourteenth century when Owain Glyndwr started making life rather hot for people in the area. The Black Canons packed up and left after nearly 300 years in residence. Not a bad record for an order formed by a debauched knight with a calling to enter the scrap metal trade.

Things were pretty quiet around Llanthony for a few hundred years. Then a bizarre Victorian poet called Walter Savage Landor bought the priory and the farm around it. Here is a sample of his work:

> Ternissa! you are fled!
> I say not to the dead,
> But to the happy ones who rest below:
> For, surely, surely, where
> Your voice and graces are,

Nothing of death can any feel or know.
 Girls who delight to dwell
 Where grows most asphodel,
Gather to their calm breasts each word you speak:
 The mild Persephone
 Places you on her knee,
And your cool palm smooths down stern Pluto's cheek.

The fact that he could make a living by writing such stuff says a lot about the Victorians. Fortunately, Walter was a contemporary of Dickens, who had the unsavoury habit of writing all his friends into his books – and a few of his enemies as well. The character called Boythorn in *Bleak House* is apparently old Walter Savage himself. He does not seem to be a very nice person at all. Here's Mr Jarndyce describing his old schoolfriend, Boythorn – alias Walter Savage Landor:

> He was then the most impetuous boy in the world, and is now the most impetuous man. He was then the loudest boy in the world and is now the loudest man . . . with his head thrown back like an old soldier, his stalwart chest squared, his hands like a clean blacksmith's and his lungs – there is no simile for his lungs. Talking, laughing or snoring they make the beams of the house shake.
>
> His language is as sounding as his voice. He is always in extremes. Perpetually in the superlative degree. In his condemnation he is all ferocity.

Such a man went down like a lead balloon with the locals, especially when he set about modernising the farm and telling them they knew nothing about farming. Walter planted the wrong sort of trees all over the place and tried to introduce Merino sheep. The trees died and the wool rotted on the sheep's backs. He soon found collecting the rent from his tenants rather difficult. He fell out with the locals left, right and centre. Landor only stayed for a few years – just long enough to lose a lot of money.

I like Llanthony Priory; it attracts interesting people.

Chapter Sixteen

Judge Jeffreys, Henry V and the head of Shakespeare

I found a field for us at the bottom of the Llanthony Valley. I had intended to stay in the tent and read, but the incessant rain-patter spattering on the flysheet drove me to spend the evening in the Skirrid, which is the oldest pub in Wales. The landlord is a phlegmatic Liverpudlian called Morris. The place does not look that old from the outside, but it certainly has atmosphere – massive black oak beams, creaking staircases and dark, beer-stained flagged floors. Alcohol has a way of stimulating the creative juices; and pubs, even quite modern ones, soon become encrusted with legends and stories. The Skirrid has been a pub for the best part of a thousand years and has accumulated more than its share of gruesome facts and fantasies. I was the first customer at the Skirrid that evening, and Morris leant on the bar retelling some of the juiciest ones in his languid Liverpudlian voice. He sounds like John Lennon with a heavy head cold. My skin started to crawl as he delivered dollops of horror. Unfortunately, the pub started to fill up with people and the spell was broken. A room full of border people hell-bent on having a good time and Bert Kaempfert and his Orchestra on the tape player are not the ideal back-drop for a ghost story. Vincent Price would have been hard-pushed to sustain the tension under such circumstances. Morris offered to give me a guided tour after closing time. I could not refuse.

I waited and drank. And drank and waited. And waited some

more. I got involved in a less than fascinating conversation with a bar bore about how the place was not what it used to be. I am sure that strangers have been exposed to similar sentiments expressed by inebriated locals since Norman times. Eventually the tide of people began to ebb. Even the bore staggered home. There were just three of us left in the bar. Morris went and turned Bert Kaempfert off and there were only two of us. Morris made coffee and we sat in one of the pews beside the remains of the fire. As we settled down, so did the building. The silence was punctuated by a steady stream of creaks and cracks and clicks. I asked Morris if the noises would stop once the place had cooled down.

'No,' he said, 'it keeps it up all night, and all day if the pub is quiet enough for you to hear. It's just like any old building,' he said, 'the beams move and shift against each other.'

I asked if we could start with the true bits about the pub. Owain Glyndwr had used it as a rallying point to muster his troops before making his assault on Brecon. Political activists have long recognised the importance of the pub as a good rallying point. The Skirrid has also done long service as the local assizes. Judge Jeffreys, the hanging judge, came here on his circuit. Trials were carried out in one of the upper rooms. Those given prison sentences were sent to Abergavenny or further afield. But in those days it was quite easy to commit a capital offence, especially when you were up before Judge Jeffreys. The records show that 183 people were hanged in the stair-well at the Skirrid. Morris sent me over to examine the marks which had been made on a beam by the hangman's rope.

The stairs were clearly visible from the bar. The condemned cell is halfway up them on the left. It is now a laundry room. It is well within earshot of the bar. Morris told me that the pub would always do a good trade on the evening before a hanging. The condemned man would have to contemplate his fate while his former neighbours whooped it up with Judge Jeffreys less than twenty feet away – giving a whole new meaning to the phrase 'being called to the bar'.

The next morning it was still raining. The weatherman gave no hint of a break in the weather. The roof of uniform grey clouds only confirmed his prediction, so I packed up in the wet, put the saddle blanket onto Molly's wet back, loaded her up and walked away from my last patch of Welsh mountains. The border swings out towards the east, swallowing up land which is flat and green and fertile enough to have been English territory. The names on the map are both English and Welsh, all jumbled up and telling a history of shifts in the position of the actual border. As we swung east, the land was still quite hilly, but it started to open out; wheat and barley appeared as the fields became big enough and flat enough to accommodate modern combine harvesters. But the cereals were only knee-high and it was still raining. The combines would not be rolling out of their sheds and barns for a few months yet.

As I walked, my over-trousers swished against each other and my hands got cold so I stopped to warm them under the blast of warm air coming out of Molly's nose as she breathed out. I stopped briefly at a pub for a pie and a pint, but I ate it outside in the drizzle, standing beside Molly. I did not want to climb out of my waterproofs and get comfortable beside the fire, only to walk out again.

It kept raining. That night I pitched the tent in the rain in a field near Monmouth. The weatherman was still gloomy about the prospects, so I decided to sit it out. I spent the next day in Monmouth. It is a nice town, but I am afraid that for me its name will always be associated with rain. Monmouth itself prefers to be associated with Henry V – as in Henry V of Agincourt, King Harry, English longbows and French knights. I have heard it said that ask any Englishman about Agincourt and he will tell you about the great battle where English technology and pluck overcame the French heavy armour. Our finest hour and all that.

Ask a Frenchman about Agincourt and all you will get is a blank look. Agincourt has been all but wiped from the French history books.

Apart from being wet, Monmouth, built where the River Monnow joins the River Wye, is also a property developer's nightmare. With river on two sides, it was a nice easy place to defend with plenty of clean, fresh running water. It was a busy town before the Romans arrived. You cannot dig a vegetable patch without turning up a few archaeological artefacts. The inhabitants of Monmouth have turned amateur archaeology into a mainstay of the town's social life. They were digging at two sites in the high street while I was there. A constant stream of townspeople were dropping in to see how the work was progressing. Every visitor put some money into the collecting box to help pay for the work which was being done in a rush to beat the developers' deadline.

The man in charge was Stephen Clarke, an unassuming sort of chap who runs the local print works. He showed me around the dig where a section of road, the floor plan of a couple of houses and a large oven of some sort had been found. Stephen and his fellow archaeologists had found a lot of potsherds and were not sure whether the oven belonged to a clumsy baker or a bad potter. Earlier on in the day, I had picked up a little book called *Ghosts of Monmouth*, by Stephen Clarke. I asked Stephen Clarke the archaeologist whether he was also Stephen Clarke the ghost-hunter. He seemed slightly embarrassed and admitted that he was. He said that he did not believe in ghosts, but the stories often had a grain of truth in them. He gave me an example which had puzzled him for a long time.

It concerned the story of a group of boys who were camping down by the river at Hadnock, not far from Monmouth. Playing around late that evening, the boys saw, down by the river, the figure of a lady walking across the meadow. She appeared to be walking along with her feet well below ground level; she was only visible from her knees up. The boys were quite close to her but none of them could make out her face.

Stephen told me that this story was just one of several he had collected for the local paper. Back in the 1960s a group of archaeologists from Monmouth were digging in the next field along. They were looking for the site of a Roman villa which they were convinced should have been there. Several weeks of digging produced nothing at all. Stephen remembered the story of the boys and decided to go and do a couple of test bores in the next field. There, a couple of feet below the surface, he found a Roman pavement. More digging produced the sought-after Roman villa and the skeleton of a woman with one side of the skull smashed in. Stephen told me the whole tale in a very matter-of-fact way with no embellishments. I asked him to tell me how such a coincidence could happen. Stephen insisted that he had no theories to explain such a thing. It was just the way things had happened, he could say no more.

I bought lots of food in town and then retreated from the drizzle to my sodden tent. I had a nice meal and settled down to read Stephen's book of ghost stories. The kettle was about half-boiled when the little meths burner ran out of fuel. I wanted that cup of coffee so I refilled the burner straight away without giving it time to cool. The box the stove came in warned me not to do anything so stupid, but I had been getting on really well with the stove. I thought that I knew better than the manufacturers what you could and could not do to it. As I poured the meths into the hot burner a little cloud of vapour rose up, ignited itself and settled on the tent flysheet. The tent started to melt and sizzle in the rain. The plastic peeled back in a sheet of flame like the map at the beginning of *Bonanza* on television. Grabbing the nearest thing I could lay my hands on, I tried to douse the flames. I could have chosen something more suitable than my plastic over-trousers. For a moment it was touch and go whether they were going to add to the conflagration. I finished that day with a hole in my tent and a hole in my over-trousers – and it was still raining.

The next day dawned dark and drizzly. I packed the wet things into the wet gear and headed off on the last full leg of the journey to the Severn Bridge and Sedbury Cliffs.

We left Monmouth at about ten in the morning and by 10.30 it had stopped raining. Everything became steamy and hot as the sun came out. I was able to abandon my waterproofs. It was good to feel the sun on my back. Molly also seemed to be happy to be released from the stable. She was positively frisky as we walked through the lanes of the Wye Valley.

It was a sunny afternoon, warm and quiet. The lanes snaked their way through patches of woodland – all that remains of the great forest which once covered the area before they started smelting iron.

The traffic was heavier than I had experienced in the northern part of the borders. At six or seven cars an hour, the lanes were still quiet when compared to Buckinghamshire, but not as empty as the ones at the start of the trip where one car every couple of hours was the norm. Oncoming cars had to stop to let us squeeze past. Those coming from behind had to wait until I could find a suitable gateway in which to park Molly. I was coming to regard car people as some sort of sub-species. Certainly they could get from place to place at an unbelievable speed – three days of packhorse travel in one hour. Given an early start in Prestatyn, which I had left over a month before, these miraculous travellers could get to Chepstow before the pubs stopped serving lunch.

But I felt sorry for the car-bound. In their cocooned existence, insulated from the wind, the smells and the sounds of the country-side, they hardly knew they were travelling. To drive from North to South Wales in a few hours would be a terrible waste – a waste of pet-rol, a waste of time, a waste of people, a waste of experience. Why bother with the cowboys at Pontin's, why stop to talk to Brother Stephen, to help Mrs Davies with her heifer, no reason to provoke a farmer into swearing at you, no Emyr Lloyd, Emyr Owens, no learn-ing about the savagery of Hopton Castle or the life of the two Ladies of Llangollen. I had gained so much over the couple of hundred miles which separate the two ends of Offa's Dyke.

It reminded me of the way that I feel when I take my dog for a walk. A walk in the country for a human being is mainly a visual pleasure; my incompetent human nose sends me only a few dulled messages, my ears offer a muffled mixture of bird-song and wind noise. The dog sees and hears things I cannot perceive.

My reveries were broken by the roar of traffic across the end of the lane I was walking along. It should have brought me into a quiet backstreet on the edge of Chepstow. There in front of me was the insane rush of traffic along the A48(T). My map-reading had clearly not been improved by six weeks on the road. I had to retrace my steps about a mile and a half – uphill. The pleasures of walking evaporated as I slogged back up the hill to get back on my proper route. It is strange how long it takes to retrace steps taken in error. I am sure that it took me the best part of forty minutes to walk back along a piece of road that only took me fifteen to travel along the first time. Molly walked more slowly as well. She somehow knew that I had wasted our time.

We picked up the route again and entered first the suburbs of Chepstow and then the town centre. I walked self-consciously through the archway in the centre of Chepstow and then down past the castle. I stopped down by the river to watch the water slooshing out of the estuary. I thought about the difficulties faced by a bizarre American called Orville Owen who expended thousands of fruitless man-hours looking for the head of Shakespeare, which he believed was buried in the bed of the River Wye. He chose a particularly hard river to excavate – the Wye happens to have the second largest tidal range of any river in the world. Dr Orville Owen was a 'Baconite' – one of a select group of people who believed that Shakespeare was not the prolific genius most of us take him to be. The theory was that somehow Shakespeare had written, or merely got hold of, a couple of good plays which sold well. His name then became thoroughly bankable, so his name was stuck on a number of other plays. Any Shakespearean scholar will tell you that, although many of the plays 'written' by Shakespeare are brilliant, there are plenty which would be better left unperformed and unwritten. The Baconites believe that the best ones were actually written by a contemporary of Shakespeare – Francis Bacon. No author could really bear to allow history to credit someone else with his work, so Bacon was supposed to have left clues scattered through the text.

Orville Owen was convinced that he had licked the problem of the hidden messages. Press cuttings from 1911 show him sitting at his 'cipher machine' as he worked out where the proof was hidden. His machine looks like two giant toilet rolls with handles at their centres so that he could spool the text in front of him. He thought that all he had to do was to come to Britain, to Chepstow in particular, take bearings from various architectural and natural features and start digging. He was convinced that he would find a hidden box telling all. A lesser mortal would have begun to doubt his theories when he found the lines crossing in the middle of the River Wye, but not Dr Owen. He spent a couple of years raising money for his great endeavour and found backers from all over the United States. Armed with loads of cash Dr Owen started digging.

Even with barriers to keep back the tide, his team only had an hour each side of low tide to do their work. They had to use the night-time low tides. Work carried on by lamplight. The bed of the Wye is made of thick black mud. It must have been an unpleasant business. Dr Owen had a very clear idea that he was looking for quite a large construction containing a number of caskets wrapped up in oiled cloth. There was also supposed to be another box containing the head of Shakespeare and some astounding revelations about Queen Elizabeth I.

Dr Owen and his efforts filled the newspapers for weeks on end. His was an ongoing story which kept readers all over the country hooked. When he first arrived, Dr Owen was treated as a highly respected academic; his ideas and aspirations were taken terribly seriously. Unfortunately for Dr Owen, the summer of 1911 was a pretty thin one for news. Dr Owen provided the perfect 'silly season' story for the hacks of Fleet Street. Gradually words such as 'eccentric' and 'quixotic' started to appear.

Then came a breakthrough. The workmen found a wooden man-made construction. The team worked at it, unearthing more and more in the brief interval they had for excavation. I can imagine Orville Owen watching the work, goading the men on, as the relentless tide came back. Then the hours spent on the river foreshore waiting for his moment of triumph, when his conviction would prevail. He must have been able to taste victory. It took several tides for the construction to be revealed as the foundations of a Roman bridge which once crossed the Wye.

The whole endeavour fell apart towards the end of July and Dr Owen returned to the United States. I wonder if he died hating the British.

With Dr Owen and his pointless endeavour in my mind, I walked on across the bridge and on towards Sedbury – a single-storey suburb of Chepstow. I walked past a massive 1950s brick-built pub where lots of teenagers were standing outside enjoying the warm evening. They eyed me suspiciously as we walked by. One of them got into his car, gunned the engine and tore off up the road with his 'Colonel Bogey' horn sounding loud in the still air. His actions created the effect he was after – it scared Molly out of her socks and impressed his friends. I calmed her down and walked on. There was a roaring

Two boys led us to the marker stone and argued about whether it was the beginning or the end of the path – one was wearing pyjamas.

behind me and he came back, cut fine across Molly's back end, and gave us another blast on his horn – producing an even more satisfying effect on the horse and the audience.

A mile further on, I joined the track to the farm where I had arranged to leave the horsebox. I had to get permission to take Molly down through the field to the marker stone at the end of the Dyke path. I asked the lady at the farm where the stone was, and she offered to send one of her sons to show me the way. His younger brother insisted on coming with us – despite the fact that he was already in his pyjamas and ready for bed. His mother forced him into his dressing gown and wellies for the trip. We must have made a bizarre little procession, the two boys, Molly and I. The boys argued about the precise location of the stone. We blundered around in the bushes for a few minutes and the boys ran off in different directions. One of them shouted that he had found it and I followed his calls to find the youngest of the two standing proudly on top of it and waving his red-checked dressing gown over his head.

I wondered out loud whether this was the beginning or the end of the path. This sparked off another disagreement between the two boys. It was a simple argument along the principle of he who shouts longest and loudest is sure to prevail. The is, isn't, is, isn't brand of discussion went on for some time before the matter was settled when the elder boy invoked the name of mother. She had apparently asserted 'just the other day' that this was the end. Pyjamas and wellies gave way to the combined authority of his elder brother and his mother.

The three of us took pictures of each other, and the time-lapse on the camera took a picture of all three plus Molly. The boys realised that it was getting dark and rushed back to the farm. I took Molly along to where the cliff dips down to the water's edge. The tide was out and there was a faint smell of sewage. Molly picked at the tough, salty grass while I watched the lights of the cars and lorries heading east across the Severn Bridge. There is something extremely odd about a journey made just for its own sake. Journeys should have a real end, a real arrival, a real reason. I have to concede that to travel on foot or horseback from Pontin's on the north coast of Wales to a patch of mud and salty grass just under the Severn Bridge is not much of an achievement. But I felt pleased, probably as pleased as that lady with the giant rucksack whom I had seen paddling at Prestatyn six weeks before. An hour later I had loaded Molly into the van and we had joined the traffic streaming across the Severn Bridge. We were heading home.

The Severn Bridge and the foreshore at the end
of the Offa's Dyke – plenty of mosquitoes and the faintest whiff of sewage.